Yesterday's Wirral
Pictorial History 1890 to 1953

INTRODUCTION

Following on from the success of our nine publications in the Yesterday's Wirral series, each covering a section of the Wirral peninsula, we have decided to publish one that encompasses all of Wirral. We have taken as a theme the many photographs from our extensive archives and included data taken from the annals section that appears at the back of Kelly's Directories and which give a brief history of local events in chronological order. We have added many other dates which have been gleaned from other local publications, newspapers etc. Many of the events are given differing facts and dates in various publications and we apologise in advance for any errors in the 1,000 plus details listed. We have also illustrated the facts with over 300 pictures and graphics and, as with all our other books, the majority of our photographs have never been published before.

We have started in 1890, as it was from around this date that local view photographs became more widespread, prior to then it was mainly portraits. We were going to finish at 1950 but decided to include the Festival of Britain in 1951 and end with the Coronation of Queen Elizabeth II in 1953.

Where possible we have acknowledged the source of the information. In addition to the dates and events gleaned from many directories, guide books, local books etc. we have sourced some details from newspaper cuttings but do not have precise details of the origins.

Design & Origination: Ian Boumphrey - Desk Top Publisher

Printed By: Printfine Ltd Liverpool L3 7HJ

Published by: Ian & Marilyn Boumphrey
The Nook 7 Acrefield Road Prenton
Wirral CH42 8LD
Tel/Fax: 0151 608 7611 e-mail: ian@yesterdayswirral.co.uk

ISBN 1-899241-15-9

£9.95

—	Alfred Harding, removals, established in **Birkenhead**	3 Apr	Presbyterian Church, Meols Drive **West Kirby** opened[HWK]
—	**New Brighton** Golf Club founded (later Warren Golf Club)	2 Jul	Blue Bell (bh) Park Street **Birkenhead** sold @ auction £1,040[LCP]
—	Freehold Methodist Chapel Old Chester Road **Birkenhead** built[OPB]	27 Nov	Plough Inn Breck Road **Poulton** sold @ auction £950[LCP]
—	**Bromborough Pool** Chapel opened[LBR]	29 Nov	YMCA moved from 42 Conway Street to new premises in Grange Road **Birkenhead**[SS]
17 Mar	*Bird in Hand* (bh) 13,14 &15 Oakdale **Seacombe** sold @ auction £2,500[LCP]		

Above: This Wirral Tramways Co Ltd horse-drawn car No. 9, along with No. 8, commenced service in 1879. They were built by the Starbuck Car and Wagon Co Ltd of Cleveland Street Birkenhead for use on their Birkenhead to New Ferry line. Although the 22 seater Nos. 1 to 9 were followed by four double-decker 42 seaters, all 13 tramcars operated until May 1900 when they were sold at auction. No. 9 was bought by Birkenhead United Tramways, Omnibus and Carriage Co Ltd, along with four others, and resumed service on the New Ferry route until they were auctioned again, in January 1901, this time for use as sheds or shelters

Below: Pictured in Birkenhead Park, either side of the two ladies, are two Russian cannons which had been captured at Sebastapol during the Crimea War in 1853. They were presented to the town of Birkenhead by the War Office in 1857. Originally sited near the main entrance to the park, they were later moved to this site which became known as Cannon Hill. In 1940 the guns together with the railings, some of which are pictured here, were taken away to be melted down as scrap for the war effort

—	Wm Bernard established in **Birkenhead**
—	**New Ferry** Methodist Church opened[LBRB]
—	Slatey Road (Park Road South) **Birkenhead** Society of Friends Church built[OPB]
—	**Heswall** Chapel Telegraph Road built[LBRB]
—	St Winifreds Welsh Church opened Westbourne Road **Birkenhead**[OPB]
—	*Bidston Court* a house in **Noctorum** built for Robert Hudson, soap manufacturer. Building moved to Royden Park in **Frankby** 1929-31 and renamed *Hillbark*
—	**Birkenhead's** *Argyle Theatre's* name restored and Dennis Clarke became sole manager
—	**Birkenhead** & District Co-op established
—	First part of promenade, from Holland Road **Seacombe** to **Egremont** Pier completed
—	*Thornton Manor* **Thornton Hough** purchased by Wm Lever
22 Jan	*White Lion Inn* (ph) **Lower Heswall** sold @ auction £4,750 [including 25 acres land in **Neston**][LCP]
5 Mar	*Shrewsbury Arms* + 2 cottages, Claughton Firs, **Oxton** sold @ auction £4,250[LCP]
9 Apr	Launch of the **Wallasey** paddle steamer, *Thistle*[KD]
11 Apr	**Meols** Golf Club started[H&WK]
15 Apr	*Birkenhead Arms* (ph) 12, Market Street **Birkenhead** + shop, house & warehouse sold @ auction £5,750[LCP]
7 May	St Saviour's C of E Church **Oxton** consecrated
15 June	Mersey Railway extension from Green Lane **Birkenhead** to **Rock Ferry** opened
2 July	First section of Manchester Ship Canal opened for traffic - **Eastham** Locks to **Ellesmere Port**
4 Aug	Market Street School **Hoylake** building opened
29 Sept	St Mark's C of E Church opened Devonshire Road **Claughton**
29 Sept	Second section of Manchester Ship Canal opened, **Ellesmere Port** to River Weaver
21 Oct	*Manor Arms* (ph) 180/2 Chester Street **Birkenhead** sold @ auction £1,605[LCP]
24 Oct	Presbyterian Mission House opened in **Seacombe**[KD]
29 Oct	**Wallasey** Golf Club links open for play
Nov	Gladstone Village Hall opened in **Port Sunlight** for the use of workers at Lever's as a dining hall and recreation hall which seated 750[KD]
28 Nov	St Andrew's Church **West Kirby** opened[H&WK]

Birkenhead & District Co-op Society established. After the first year membership was 315 with sales over £4,100[OPB]

The YMCA building in Grange Road, which was erected in 1890 at a cost of £10,000, was built in the Renaissance style of terra cotta. It contained a large public hall holding 900 people [see Baden Powell's speech here in 1908], a gymnasium with lavatories, hot & cold baths, also a reading room, reference library and classroom[KD]

Population at 1891 Census

Arrowe	128
Barnston	404
Bebington Hr	4,372
Bebington Lr	5,216
Bidston	254
Birkenhead	58,287
Brimstage	199
Bromborough	1,662
Burton	266
Caldy	170
Capenhurst	158
Childer Thornton	743
Claughton-cum-Grange	3,510
Eastham	1,729
Frankby	221
Gayton	199
Grange	156
Greasby	237
Heswall-cum-Oldfield	1,210
Hoose	1,658
Hooton	537
Irby	174
Landican	76
Ledsham	83
Leighton	325
Liscard	16,323
Meols, Great	456
Meols, Little	1,962
Moreton-cum-Lingham	464
Ness	354
Neston, Great	2,240
Little Neston	1,012
Noctorum	202
Overpool	112
Oxton	4,429
Pensby	51
Poulton-cum-Seacombe	14,839
Poulton-cum-Spital	489
Prenton	267
Puddington	150
Raby	339
Saughall Massie	189
Shotwick	77
Storeton	256
Sutton, Great	395
Sutton, Little	1,094
Thingwall	173
Thornton Hough	487
Thurstaston	145
Tranmere	30,680
Upton	687
Wallasey	2,067
West Kirby	2,441
Whitby	5,107
Willaston	502
Woodchurch	129

1892

—	Basketball introduced into **Birkenhead** YMCA. Game originated in America in 1891
9 Jan	Charles Thompson Mission's new premises opened in Hemingford Street, **Birkenhead** which was formerly a Quaker Meeting Place [the Mission is still there today][PHB]
26 Jan	**Birkenhead** Lawn Tennis Club founded
24 Feb	First Cyclist's Carnival at **Wallasey**[KD]
20 May	Tower of St Saviours Church **Oxton** dedicated
21 May	Recreation Ground opened in **New Brighton**[KD]
26 May	Christian Institute opened in Grange Road, **West Kirby**[H&WK]
26 May	Ship Inn, + shop **Heswall** sold @ auction £1,700[LCP]
31 May	New **Seacombe** railway line opened and double line to **Hoylake** opened from **Bidston**[H&WK]
24 June	**Liscard** Baptist Chapel opened[KD]
13 Jul	Smithy + 2 cottages, Hope Street **New Brighton** sold £450[LCP]
18 Jul	First county cricket match at **Birkenhead** Park Cheshire v Derbyshire[WBD]
27 Jul	**Wallasey** Band Stand opened[KD]
23 Aug	*Stanley Arms Hotel* + bowling green, Victoria Road **Seacombe** sold @ auction £11,500[LCP]
Sept	The adjoining *Black Bull & Greenland Fisheries* **Neston** were both acquired and merged by a Chester brewery and became the *Greenland Fisheries*[BW]
26 Sept	Birkenhead Pavilion & Roller Skating Rink opened in Park Road East **Birkenhead**[BW]
Oct	**Birkenhead** Park Rugby Club new pavilion built[BW]
18 Oct	**Seacombe** Congregational Church & School - foundation stone laid[KD]
5 Nov	Battleship *Royal Oak* launched at Cammell Laird **Birkenhead**[MOI]
22 Nov	The Charles Dawson Brown Museum opened at St Bridget's Church **West Kirby**[H&WK]
13 Dec	Seacombe Promenade Recreation Ground open to the public[KD]
24 Dec	**Wallasey** Golf Club house opened

Chevalier T.H. Crowther was the star attraction at the Birkenhead Royal Pavilion, Elite Skating Rink, opposite the main entrance to Birkenhead Park, for the week commencing 31 October 1892. Although with a foreign sounding name and foreign accent, he was born in Bradford. He gave an interview in his rooms at the Queens Hotel, next to the rink, to the Birkenhead Wasp where he related his fascinating, adventurous life story. Known as the King of Skaters, he had travelled in every country except Australia. One of his most daring feats was to ride a bicycle across Niagara Falls in America on a plank of wood nine inches wide in front of an audience of 10,000 people. In Mexico he engaged in a bull fight riding a high bicycle and also saved a young tiger cat from an attack by a snake. He had performed in front of many of the world's Royalty and was off to Paris the following week to perform on a new ice skating rink for a salary of 200 francs a night (then £200!). Needless to say he got rave revues in the local press for his performance in Birkenhead[BW]

Left: Paddle Steamer Snowdon was built in 1892 by Laird Bros at Birkenhead for the Snowdrop Passenger Steamship Co. She was a two-funnelled Saloon Paddler which carried a certificate for 462 passengers and had a speed of 14 knots. Used as a minesweeper based at Dover and Harwich during the First World War which she survived and then resumed her North Wales services in 1919. Finally she was broken up at Port Glasgow in 1931[WCS]

THESE ADVERTISEMENTS ARE TAKEN
FROM *MEMORIES OF BIRKENHEAD*
by HILDA GAMLIN 1892

ALBERT COLE & CO.

Family Grocers, Provision Merchants and
Italian Warehousemen,

BIRKENHEAD & ROCK FERRY

TELEPHONE No. 4113.

A WELL-SELECTED STOCK OF

CHINA, INDIA AND CEYLON TEAS

Now on hand,

ALSO THE SPECIAL TEA FOR CONNOISSEURS,

GOLDEN TIPS, 4/- per lb.

MOCHA, EAST INDIA AND PLANTATION CEYLON COFFEES

ROASTED AND GROUND DAILY.

FRESH NORMANDY AND DANISH BUTTER.	CHOICE CUMBERLAND AND ISLE OF WIGHT HAMS.
WILTSHIRE AND WATERFORD BACON.	THE BEST BRANDS OF ENGLISH AND AMERICAN OX TONGUES.
CHEDDAR, GORGONZOLA & GRUYERE CHEESE.	MELTON MOWBRAY PIES.

Dessert Specialities.

CARLSBAD & ELVAS PLUMS.	CRYSTALLIZED FRUITS.
CLUSTERS MUSCATEL RAISINS.	FRUITS, FOURRES.
ELEME FIGS.	CARAMELS, WALNUTS.
VERY FINE TAFILAT DATES.	MARRONS GLACE.
1-LB. BOXES TUNIS DATES.	COMPAGNIE CHOCOLAT.
NORMANDY PIPPINS.	ROWNTREE'S CHOCOLAT.
	CREMES AND NOUGATS.

WEST INDIA DRIED TURTLE.	CORALLINE PEPPER.
COCKS' COMBS.	TRUFFLES. FOIS GRAS.
RAGOUT FINANCIERE.	NORWEGIAN LAX.
NUJEEB KHAN CHUTNEYS.	OLIVES, FARCIES
TOBASCO SAUCE.	FINEST RUSSIAN CAVIARE.

Albert Cole & Co at the time of this advertisements had
branches at 10/12 Grange Road & 141 Price Street
Birkenhead and 482 New Chester Road, Rock Ferry. The
business dates back to at least 1877 when their premises
were at 10/12 Grange Road & 127 Price Street
Birkenhead and Rock Ferry Pier. However by 1896 the
business is no longer mentioned in Gores Directory

[I wonder how one ate Cocks' Combs?]

MRS. JAMES

Servants' Registry Appointment Rooms

36 GRANGE ROAD WEST,

BIRKENHEAD.

Superior Servants waiting to be engaged.

HOPE & LEE

MERCHANT TAILORS

Boys' Clothiers, Outfitters, Hosiers & Hatters,

17 & 19 CROSS STREET,

104 & 106 CHESTER STREET,

AND WEST END BRANCH—

88 GRANGE ROAD,

BIRKENHEAD.

TERMS CASH.

Another well known **Birkenhead** family business was
started in 1864 when John Lee set up his first shop. By
1877 he had joined with Joseph Hope, trading as Hope &
Lee. Although the partnership did not survive long, the
name was retained and continued trading until the 1980s

HUBBARD & MARTIN

WHOLESALE AND RETAIL

Bakers, Confectioners, and Public Caterers

11 & 12 MARKET PLACE SOUTH
45 BOROUGH ROAD
243 GRANGE ROAD, CHARING CROSS

BIRKENHEAD.

AND 108 BEDFORD ROAD,

ROCK FERRY.

VANS TO ALL PARTS OF TOWN AND SUBURBS DAILY.

HUBBARD & MARTIN.

Mr JJ Martin (a Chemist form Malden, Essex) moved to
Birkenhead and with his brother, Ralph, in
1880: opened a Bakery at 45, Borough Road, on the
corner of Rodney Street, **Birkenhead**.
1886: Mr CH Hubbard (also originating from Malden)
opened a Bakery at 12, Market Street South, Birkenhead
in partnership with a Mr Handley (his father-in-law) -
trading as Hanley & Hubbard.
1889: Mr CH Hubbard and Mr JJ Martin joined forces
trading as Hubbard & Martin (their wives were daughters
of Mr CH Hubbard's former partner Mr Handley) with
their first branch at 12 Market Place South, Birkenhead.
Three years later they operated from the branches listed
above and by 1900 business was so good they opened a
purpose built Electric Bakery in Pilgrim Street
Birkenhead.
The company continued to prosper, with many branches in
the Birkenhead area, and was eventually taken over in the
1950s by Thos Scott & Sons (Bakers) Ltd of Liverpool

—	Temporary Laird Street Council School opened in **Birkenhead**[WBD]
—	Wm Lever replaced old, unhealthy cottages with new at **Thornton Hough**
—	**Whitby** C of E infants school opened in Arrowe Lane
23 Jan	The School board, having taken over the old Mission School in **Seacombe,** opened its first board school (Somerville Council School)[KD]
3 Apr	Memorial stone laid - Methodist Free Church **Seacombe**[KD]
3 Jun	Wesleyan Chapel Foundation stone laid at **Liscard**[KD]
17 Oct	*The Wheatsheaf* (ph) **Ness** sold @ auction £2,100[LCP]
14 Dec	**Liscard** Wesleyan Chapel opened in Manor Road[KD]

The *Seven Stars Hotel* is pictured at Thornton Hough in 1893 when Frederick Osborne was the then victualler of this Birkenhead Brewery public house

Left: Members of Hoylake Bowling Club are pictured in front of the pavilion which was situated at the rear of the Stanley Hotel Market Street **Hoylake**

Below: A view of four cottages in Neston Road **Thornton Hough,** at the junction of Smithy Hill, c.1890, which were to be replaced by the houses built on this site facing the Village Green in 1893. The signpost points left to Willaston and back to Neston. Wm. Lever acquired, by degrees, the greater part of the village of Thornton Hough. The exteriors of some of the old thatched, whitewashed cottages were picturesque. However, the interiors were dark, damp and unhealthy. In one of these cottages, consisting of one living-room and one bedroom, a farm labourer and his wife had brought up a family of twelve children. They were eventually persuaded to move into one of the newly-built houses in the village

—	**New Brighton** Chapel built Seabank Road[LBRB]
—	Two **Birkenhead** Branch libraries opened - North branch in Price Street, **Birkenhead** & South branch in Grove Road, **Rock Ferry**
—	Della Robbia Pottery formed in **Birkenhead**
—	**Leasowe** Railway Station opened[PWR]
—	Building the new Royal Liverpool Golf Club house commenced at **Hoylake** [RLGC] Well sunk on a site near Seaview Road to supply the increase in demand for water in **Wallasey.**
6 Jan	International rugby union match held @ **Birkenhead** Park England v Wales
Feb	Wirral Ladies Golf Club instituted in **Bidston**
19 Feb	*Derby Arms* (ph) + workshops etc, Nelson Road, **Rock Ferry**, sold @ auction £4,600[LCP]
Apr	**Hoylake** Urban District Council formed
27 Apr	First portion of **Bidston** Hill acquired by Birkenhead Corporation
22 May	**New Brighton** Convalescence Home opened[KD]
21 May	Manchester Ship Canal opened by Queen Victoria
14 Jun	Stone Quarry, Holt Hill, **Tranmere** sold @ auction £305[LCP]
1 July	Mersey Docks & Harbour Board handed over all Lifeboat Stations to the RNLI[HLA]
3 Aug	Grand opening of Lipton's Provision Market at 168 Grange Road, **Birkenhead**[MB]
Oct	Kirby Park Station opened on the Hooton to **West Kirby** line[H&WK] **Caldy** Cross erected on Ascension Day
1 Nov	St John's Church **Egremont** re-opened after extension[KD]

The idea for the establishment of Wirral Ladies Golf Club originated from members of the Royal Liverpool Golf Club for their wives, who were very keen, as the Hoylake club would not then admit ladies. Land on Oxton Heath in Bidston Road, Bidston, was initially leased from the Earl of Shrewsbury and a nine hole course opened at Easter 1895. The club was run by ladies with men only admitted as associate members. By 1907 the course had been increased to 18 holes and in 1927 the club was able to purchase the land for £17,000[YW2]

Above: The three-horse omnibus of the Birkenhead United Tramways, Omnibus and Carriage Company is passing Bradbury's Ironmongers shop at No.90 Oxton Road on the corner of Mornington Street **Birkenhead**. One of the advantages of the omnibus was that it was not confined by rails so was able to travel without restriction, unlike the tram. The passengers on this omnibus could either travel inside, or weather permitting, sit on the top deck. However, the poor driver had no option and had to sit out in all weathers[TBW]

Hoylake had two lighthouses - Lower and Upper - the lower is seen left c.1894 with the upper one pictured right. The Lower Lighthouse, which was sited off Alderley Road facing the sea, was the third one on this site, built in 1865. The light was last lit on 14 July 1908. It then became the entrance to the Lighthouse Pavilion but the lighthouse was demolished in December 1922. The lifeboat house pictured here was the one rebuilt in 1837, replacing the original one which dated back to 1803, to house two boats. In 1897 the Hoylake Urban District Council decided to build a promenade along the front at Hoylake. However, the lifeboat house was in the way and the

Council negotiated with the RNLI, who had taken over the building in 1894, to demolish the old shed and contribute £200 towards the cost of a new one as well as building a launch-way from the new lifeboat house which cost £922 opening in 1899.

The Upper Lighthouse at Hoylake, pictured right in Valencia Road c.1894, was built in 1865 and last lit on 14 May 1886. During the Second World War, the upper lighthouse was used an an observation post by the Royal Observer Corps. The building still exists today as part of a private dwelling

— St Michaels & All Angels **Claughton** built[OPB]
— Woodland Junior Mixed & Infants School opened in Borough Road **Birkenhead**[OPB]
— Royal Liverpool Golf Club moved from their headquarters in the *Royal Hotel* to their new clubhouse in Meols Drive **Hoylake** which cost £8,000[RLGC]
— **Birkenhead** Fire Station opened in Whetstone Lane
— Lifeboat service taken over by the Royal National Lifeboat Institution from the Mersey Docks & Harbour Board[H&WD]
— **Hoylake** Ladies Golf Club founded - 18 holes
— **Wallasey** Co-operative Society amalgamated with Birkenhead Co-operative Society

1 Jan　Branch railway line from **Bidston** to **Seacombe & Egremont** opened with intermediate stations at **Liscard and Poulton**

23 Jan　*Great Britain* (ph), 15 King Street, **Egremont**, sold @ auction £7,750[LCP]

Feb　River Mersey froze in parts & ice flows floated down the river *(see picture below)*

3 Feb　Fire at Congregational Church, **Liscard**[KD]

10 Mar　**Birkenhead** Infectious Diseases Hospital opened inTollemache Road (see below)[KD]

10 April　Removal of "Noah's Ark", a wrecked boat, from **New Brighton** beach[KD]

25 May　Girl's camp at **Wallasey** opened[KD]

3 July　Destructor opened at Wallasey[KD]

5 July　Disastrous fire at Buchanan's Flour Mills, **Seacombe**[KD]

13 July　Foundation stone laid for Christ Church, **Port Sunlight**[KD]

8 Nov　*Graving Dock Hotel* (ph) in **Birkenhead** sold @ auction £8,550[LCP]

11 Dec　Stone quarry, Telegraph Road, **Heswall**, sold @ auction £500[LCP]

11 Dec　Smithy & workshop, The Village, **Lower Heswall**, sold @ auction £8,550[LCP]

Birkenhead Infectious Diseases Hospital was opened in Tollemache Road, Birkenhead 10 March 1895

Royal Liverpool Golf Club at **Hoylake,** which was founded in 1869, had used part of the Royal Hotel as its headquarters. In 1879 an extension was built onto the hotel including a club room, other accodommation and also a caddies' quarters for which the club signed a 15 year lease. In 1894, one year before the lease was up, it was decided they should have a new purpose-built club house. Following a competition Messrs Woodfall & Eccles's design was chosen and the new clubhouse was opened in Meols Drive in 1895 at a cost of £8,000[RLGC]

Below: This view of the Lighthouse and Fort at **New Brighton** was taken in February 1895 when large ice-floes had come down from the upper reaches of the River bringing small icebergs. At low tide the Mersey had the appearance of a vast ice field which remained for a few weeks before the thaw set in

—	Park Road Baptist Church Whetstone Lane **Birkenhead** built[OPB]
—	Harry Lauder first appeared at the Argyle Theatre **Birkenhead**
—	**Puddington** Methodist Chapel built[OPB]
—	**New Brighton** Graydon Castle Great Wheel & Tower Co Ltd purchase the Palace with the intention of building the world's largest wheel on the site
—	New railway station built at **West Kirby**[POR]
—	**Rock Ferry** FC founded, used a ground in Bedford Park[TR1]
—	St Winifred's Welsh Church, Westbourne Road, **Birkenhead** consecrated[OPB]
—	Victoria Hotel New Brighton re-opened
23 Jan	**Wallasey** Local Board accepts Messrs. Harrison's gift of the new Harrison Park
28 Mar	Fire at St James' Church **New Brighton**[KD]
28 Mar	Mr WE Gladstone opened the Wirral Railway for goods traffic[PWR]
18 May	**Bidston** to Harwarden railway line opened to passengers. Intermediate stations at: **Neston, Storeton and Upton**[POR]
12 Jun	Launch of the *John Heron* - one of the last two **Wallasey** Ferry paddle steamers[WCS]
22 June	First sod cut for **New Brighton** Tower Grounds
24 Jun	Dedication of organ St Mary's Church **Liscard**
Aug	Plot of land in Telegraph Road **Heswall** opposite the Puddydale, was purchased for £500 by the Presbyterian Church of England and the "Tin Tabernacle" erected on the site
Sep	**Leasowe** Castle sold @ auction £7,000 and opened as the fully licensed *Leasowe Castle Hotel*[LCP]
Sep	**Birkenhead** Corporation commence to supply electricity[B]
1 Sep	Toll on **Poulton** Bridge increased from one half penny to one penny
8 Sep	**Egremont** Baptist Schools opened
2 Oct	Launch of the last **Wallasey** Paddle Steamer Pansy[WCS]
10 Oct	Consecration of Christ Church, **Liscard**
9 Nov	**Birkenhead's** Argyle Theatre showed films – reputed to be the first time outside London[RP]

This advertisement was taken from a programme for a "Grand Entertainment by the Kentucky Darkies Amateur Minstrel Society" in Aid of St Werburgh's RC School, Birkenhead Wednesday 15 April 1896

This 1896 photograph is looking down Hamilton Street towards Hamilton Square, Birkenhead. The original top to the Town Hall can be seen on the right. This was destroyed by fire in 1901 and replaced. The shop below the clock is on the corner of Market Street

This panoramic view of Hoylake was taken a few years before the promenade was built. Trinity Road is to the left of the left mast. The Lower and Upper Lighthouses can be seen to the right with the old Lifeboat House on the extreme right. This was replaced in 1899 with the present one

—	Holy Trinity Cof E School Eldon Street **Birkenhead** opened[WBD]
—	Birkenhead Council purchased **Rock Ferry & New Ferry** cross-river services
—	Commencement of the promenade extension from Holland Road, to beyond **New Brighton** pier
—	**Wallasey** Council purchased the Earlston Estate for £20,000 - the site of Earlston Library
—	Victoria Hall, Hr **Bebington** was erected in The Village at a cost of £1,850
—	Liscard Fire Station opened
—	Marine Park, **New Brighton**, opened
—	New Brighton Tower grounds opened
—	Royal Liverpool Golf Club **Hoylake** hosted the Open Championship - won by HH Hilton member of RLGCRLGC
—	St Stephen's Church Prenton Lane **Prenton** dedicated building cost £10,000
—	**Wallasey** School of Art opened
—	**West Kirby** Public Hall opened in Grange Road Jan Generating station opened in Sea View Road, supplying the first electricity in **Wallasey**
Apr	Branch of The Bank of Liverpool opened at **West Kirby**
30 Apr	Union Hotel **Parkgate** sold @ auction £5,100[LCP]
26 May	Mr James Lever died. He was father of the founders of Lever Bros Port Sunlight[KD]
18 Jun	**Birkenhead** Park staged a celebration for Queen Victoria's Diamond Jubilee
19 Jun	12,000 Birkenhead children walked in procession, during heavy rain, to celebrate Queen Victoria's Jubilee[WBD]
22 Jun	A Grand Marine display on River Mersey to celebrate Queen Victoria's Jubilee[KD]
14 Jul	Victoria Park **Ellesmere Port** opened
18 Jul	St Agnes' Roman Catholic Church, Darmonds Green **West Kirby** opened[DOS]
2 Sep	**Birkenhead** Corporation acquired over 62 acres on Bidston Hill[B]
23 Sep	**Egremont** Pier wrecked by storm
17 Dec	Steam Fire Engine The Napier purchased

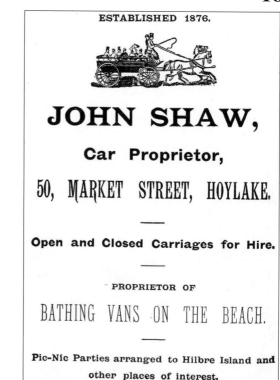

ESTABLISHED 1876.

JOHN SHAW,

Car Proprietor,

50, MARKET STREET, HOYLAKE.

Open and Closed Carriages for Hire.

PROPRIETOR OF

BATHING VANS ON THE BEACH.

Pic-Nic Parties arranged to Hilbre Island and other places of interest.

The front view of *Mayer Hall* (above) in **Bebington** Village was where the Library was founded in 1866 by Joseph Mayer who purchased a farm with a large barn attached, in five acres of land. A clock tower was erected at the front of the building and the grounds behind became a public park. A small museum was housed here at one time. The rear view of *Pennant House,* Mr Mayer's home which became the municipal offices, is seen below. Both photos were copied from glass slides taken in the 1890s[SB]

The Paddle Steamer Pearl was built by J Jones (Liverpool) in 1897. It operated on the service from **Eastham** to Liverpool until 1928 and from 1901 to 1914 it also called at **Rock Ferry**

THESE ADVERTISEMENTS WERE TAKEN FROM THE
"HOYLAKE & WEST KIRBY DIRECTORY of 1897"

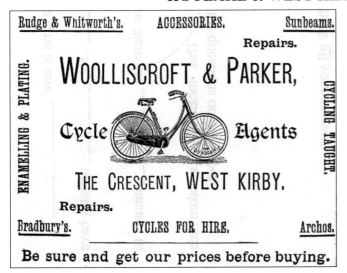

Rudge & Whitworth's.   ACCESSORIES.   Sunbeams.
Repairs.

WOOLLISCROFT & PARKER,

ENAMELLING & PLATING.

Cycle ——— Agents

CYCLING TAUGHT.

THE CRESCENT, WEST KIRBY.

Repairs.

Bradbury's.   CYCLES FOR HIRE.   Archos.

Be sure and get our prices before buying.

John Shaw (top left) not only hired out carriages but operated the bathing vans on the beach at Hoylake (where ladies could change into swim wear and be wheeled out into the sea to bath in relative privacy!)

Wooliscroft & Parker's premises were 15 The Crescent West Kirby

Mrs Blades first class Ladies & Children's outfitters was situated at Osborne House Hoylake

James Campbell, Saddler, was based at 30 Market Street

John (Jack) Morris opened the club shop in the stables of the Royal Hotel, Stanley Road when the Royal Liverpool Golf Club was founded in 1869, using the hotel as its headquarters. Morris moved his shop with the club to the new club house on Meols Drive in 1895[RLGC]

Mrs. BLADES,
Osborne House, Hoylake

FIRST-CLASS

Ladies' and Children's Outfittin

HOSIERY & BABY LINEN ESTABLISHMENT.

CB., S.S., S.P., and all well-known makes kept in stock or made to order.

makes kept in stock or made to order.

THE S&S DENECIA Long Waisted Reef CORSET.

The Celebrated Hibernian and Sterling Underclothing.
ALL GOODS OF THE BEST MANUFACTURE.
LADIES' SHIRTS AND BLOUSES.   Perfect Fittin
Established to supply the Best Articles at Fair Prices.   Ladies will find
Mrs. Blades' Stock will bear comparison with any House in Liverpool.
Agent for P. & P. Campbell, Perth Dye Works, and Atlas Delive

SADDLERY & PORTMANTEAU DEPOT,
MARKET ST., HOYLAKE.

WHIPS,
STABLE BROOMS,
BASKETS,
COMBS, &c.

SPONGES,
CHAMOIS SKINS,
DANDIES,
WATER AND BODY
BRUSHES.

JAMES M. CAMPBELL,

SADDLER,

Portmanteau, Ladies' Dress Basket
and Cabin Trunk Maker.

TRUNKS & PORTMANTEAUS REPAIRED.

New Locks and Keys fitted to Trunks.
Rug and Portmanteau Straps, in stock or
made to order.

AGENT FOR MORRIS'S
GOLF CLUBS AND BALLS.

ESTABLISHED 1869.
——

JOHN MORRIS,

WHOLESALE AND RETAIL

GOLF CLUB & BALL

MANUFACTURER,

HOYLAKE, CHESHIRE.

——

CLUBS, all made from the best
selected wood.

——

Golf Bags and all necessaries in
stock or to order.

— **Irby** Mill, a post mill erected on a brick base between 1709–25 said to have been demolished in 1898 (see photograph opposite)
— **Liscard** Fire Station opened[KD]
— Adeler & Sutton's Pierrot Troupe perform their first of many seasons on **New Brighton** Pier
— Ford water pumping station opened near Upton Station
— *Liscard Vale* and *The Woodlands* **New Brighton** purchased by the council for £11,250[KD]
— **New Brighton** Tower Theatre opened[KD]
— Riverside School **Egremont** opened
— **Wallasey** Corporation completed the purchase of the 31.5 acres of land for the cemetery at Rake Lane[KD]
— Perch Rock Battery **New Brighton** re-armed with modern guns[FPR]

21 Jan   Princess Louise & Marquis of Lorne visit **Birkenhead**[WBD]
2 Feb   Hoylake Town Hall opened
Mar   Marine Park, **New Brighton** opened to the public[KD]
3 Mar   Mersey Docks & Harbour Board resolve to spend £24,000 in extending **Wallasey** Landing Stage[KD]
1 May   **Heswall Hills** Railway Station opened[PWR]
11 Mar   Beaver Liner Lake Winnipeg collided with **Seacombe** stage[KD]
Aug   Atlantic Hotel (ph), 255 Price Street, **Birkenhead** + lock-up shop sold @ auction £12,500[LCP]
21 Oct   Marble bust of John Laird unveiled Hamilton Square, **Birkenhead**[KD]
14 Dec   The Great Eastern Picnic Hotel, **New Ferry** Road **New Ferry** sold @ auction £8,400[LCP]

Keenan's Cottage is pictured in Mill Lane, **Liscard** in 1898. It was named after its occupant a Mr Harry Keenan who was caretaker of the water tower opposite, part of which was originally used by the fire brigade. The key was obtained from Harry Keenan when the fire alarm was raised and a pull-cord sounded the bell at the top of the tower. This alerted the volunteer firemen who would hasten down to their station.
This thatched cottage was demolished *c.*1912[YW5]

HOYLAKE & WEST KIRBY PUBLIC OFFICES & TOWN HALL

[This Engraving is a reduction from the Large Plate presented with "HERALD AND VISITOR" of 27th March 1897

GENERAL DESCRIPTION from the " HERALD & VISITOR."

These buildings are now in course of erection on a site at the junction of Market Street with Albert Road, Hoylake, from the designs of Mr. Thomas W. Cubbon, Architect, of Birkenhead, who obtained first premium in our open competition.

The entrance to Public Offices is from Market Street, to the right of which the Town Clerk's, Medical Officer's Department, and Council Chamber are arranged, the Surveyor's and Rate Collector's Departments being on the left.

The Fire Station fronts Albert Road, and consists of engine house, assembly room and large yard. The remaining portion of ground floor is arranged for Technical Classes, &c. The first floor consists mainly of large Public Hall, capable of accommodating about 500 people, three entrances being provided, one from Market Street and two from Albert Road. Ladies' and gentlemen's dressing rooms and large refreshment room are arranged in connection with Hall. The Caretaker's House is over the Fire Station and is approached from Albert Road.

The buildings will be faced with red Ruabon bricks with dressings of Runcorn stone and terra cotta. The Fire Station and Technical block have been carried out by Messrs. Hill & Co., of Woolton, Liverpool, and a tender for Public Offices and Hall, submitted by W. H. Forde of Birkenhead, has been accepted. The total cost of Buildings will be about £5,000.

Hoylake Town Hall opened 2 February 1898 and the above article appeared in the Hoylake & West Kirby Directory of 1897

This close-up view of **Irby** Mill, a post mill erected on a brick base between 1709-25, was probably taken in 1898, the year that it is said to have been demolished. Local legend had it that behind the demolition was the miller, who wanted this dilapidated mill taken down but who would not pay to have it done professionally. He hired two men from a local pub to do the deed. However, as they were no experts in demolition matters, they removed the brick base without first propping up the upper part - hence there was a creaking noise and the whole structure gradually began to move, then slowly topple. This gave the men enough warning and the miller looking out of the cottage window saw the two men running for their lives, they just escaped and were never seen again! [Whether this story is fact or fiction – one thing is sure that the windmill was demolished.]
The miller's cottage in the background became *The Old Mill Cafe* (see 1924) and eventually formed part of *The Mill* pub which opened in 1980

Children are pictured enjoying themselves on **New Brighton** beach. New Brighton Pier is in the background and below the sign for 'Oysters' on the right is the lower part of the 'Ham & Egg Parade' (see 1906). Many of the Victorian ladies are dressed in black

—	Well Lane Council School **Rock Ferry** opened[WBD]
—	**Hoylake** Promenade completed in spring
—	**Hoylake** Chapel Market Street built[LBRB]
—	Foundation stone laid of Emmanuel Church **New Brighton**
—	**Hoylake** Lifeboat Station completed cost £922
—	**Liscard** Hall Estate purchased (now Central Park)
30 Jan	Opening of Vernon's Flour Mills Seacombe[KD]
4 Feb	**Rock Ferry**/ Liverpool ferry service commenced
1 May	St Hilderburgh's Church **Hoylake** opened
20 May	Vale Park **Egremont** opened[KD]
30 May	*Old Red Lion Inn* (ph) **Little Sutton** sold @ auction £5,500[LCP]
30 Jun	Triangular ferry service commenced Rock **Ferry/New Ferry** /Liverpool
6 Jul	Foundation stone laid for New Central Hospital, **Liscard**[KD]
16 Jul	Holy Name of Jesus RC Church, Beresford Road, **Oxton** opened[DoS]
19 Jul	Duke of York distributed prizes won by *HMS Conway* cadets
1 Aug	**Burton** Point Station opened[PWR]
21 Sep	St Hildeburgh's Church Stanley Road, **Hoylake**, consecrated[HMP]
Oct	The Arudy Estate, Bebington Road **Hr Tranmere** comprising *The Towers & Rockleigh House* sold @ auction £11,350[LCP]
5 Oct	Foundation stone laid for new **Wallasey** Mission Hall[KD]
21 Oct	Marine Lake **West Kirby** opened[YW3]
21 Oct	Foundation stone laid for St Luke's Chapel of Ease **Poulton**[KD]

Nov	**Ellesmere Port** & District Co-op Society formed[EP]
3 Nov	First issue of *Wallasey News*[WON]
13 Nov	**West Kirby** Public Hall opened
23 Nov	Chairman of White Star Line, Thomas Ismay, died and was buried at **Thurstaston**[Th]
18 Dec	Irving Theatre opened in Victoria Road (later became Borough Road) **Seacombe**[KD]
30 Dec	Recreation Ground opened in St Paul's Road **Seacombe**[KD]

Right: Timetable for the **Rock Ferry, New Ferry** & Liverpool ferry service from 1 August 1899 when a return ticket to Liverpool from either New Ferry or Rock Ferry would cost two pence (1p)
Below: *The Old Red Lion* Chester Road, **Little Sutton,** was sold at auction by the Little Sutton Loyal Victoria Lodge of Oddfellows on 30 May 1899. This public house was purchased by West Cheshire Brewery for £5,500. It is pictured here in the early years of the 20th century when Walter Duckworth was the victualler[LCP]

Above: The original part of *Liscard Vale House* (seen above) which dates back to the early 1840s, is the two storied part of the building on the left The extensions either side of the original building were built for one of its early owners, a Charles Holland, who purchased the property in 1844 and, due to his large family of nine children plus servants, extended the property; Holland Road is named after the family.

He died in 1870 and his widow in 1892. *Liscard Vale House* was sold to a David Benno Rappart in June 1898 for a total of £7,000 who five months later sold the property on to the Wallasey Urban District Council for £7,750.

The Council opened up the grounds of *Liscard Vale House* and also the grounds of Woodlands to the public on 20 May 1899 renaming it Vale Park. Part of *Liscard Vale House* become a cafe for visitors and *Woodlands* was demolished shortly after. The park is famous for its bandstand

Left: The *Irving Theatre,* which was built on the site of *Hope House* and its garden, was opened in Victoria Road, **Seacombe** (later to become Borough Road), by Sir Henry Irving, the distinguished actor whom it was named after, on 18 December 1899. He agreed to his name being used providing only serious theatre was performed there. The theatre was closed for several months following a fire in 1908. When it reopened it had changed its name to the *Kings Theatre* as it had been decided to show music hall acts which would contravene the personal agreement with Sir Henry Irving

—	Riverside Board School opened in Demesne Street **Seacombe**[LBRB]
—	St Paul's Presbyterian Church North Road **Tranmere** built[OPB]
—	Birkenhead Corporation extended electric supply to **Bidston & Noctorum**[WBD]
—	Opening of new **Wallasey** Central Police Station @ cost £11,000 (see picture below)[KD]
—	**New Brighton** Tower opened[KD]
—	Livingstone Street Baths **Birkenhead** opened[WBD]
—	SS*Lily* passenger ferry steamer launched[WCS]
—	SS*Rose* passenger ferry steamer launched[WCS]
—	Presbyterian Church opened in **Wallasey Village**[KD]
—	St Joseph RC Church North Road **Birkenhead** opened[DoS]
—	Wesley Hall **Liscard** opened[KD]
—	VictoriaCentral Hospital **Liscard** Bazaar raised £5,400[MM]
14 Jan	New Pentecostal Church opened at **Liscard**[KD]
Feb	*York Hotel Price Street, Park View Hotel* Price Street & *Charing Cross Hotel* Grange Road West **Birkenhead** sold £37,000[LCP]
15 Feb	St Elizabeth's Convent Park Road north **Birkenhead** opened[DoS]
28 Feb	In the Boer War Ladysmith was relieved and the **Moreton** C of E School hoisted the Union Jack and sang *Soldiers of the Queen*
24 Mar	**Wallasey** Central Library opened in Earlston Hall[KD]
1 April	Riverside Board School opened in Demesne Street **Seacombe**[KD]
7 April	*Bulls Head Inn,* (ph), **Great Sutton** sold £1,700[LCP]
7 May	Mafeking relieved - great rejoicings
11 May	**Upton** Presbyterian Church of England Ford Road - new church officially opened[OPB]
26 May	Memorial Stone laid for Welsh Church, **Liscard**[KD]
3 Aug	**Birkenhead** Agricultural Show @ **Bidston** wrecked by gales[WBD]
9 Sept	The caretaker of Conway Street Post Office in **Birkenhead**, George Fell, was found murdered – case remains unsolved[MMB]
20 Oct	Great fire of **Seacombe** - oil mills burnt down[KD]

This Lever's advert for *Monkey Brand* soap with a Boer War theme appeared in the 17 March 1900 edition of *The Sphere*

The Wheatsheaf Inn at **Raby Mere**, pictured here around the turn of the century, dates back to 1611. Situated on the connecting road from Birkenhead across Wirral to Neston, this thatched hostelry must have been a welcome sanctuary for weary travellers in days gone by.

Left: Wallasey Central Police Station opened in Manor Road – cost £11,000[KD]

New Brighton Tower and Recreation Grounds

These magnificent grounds, which cost upwards of half-a-million pounds sterling, were opened to the public on Whit Monday 1897.

The Tower, which is the highest structure in the kingdom, stands 621 feet above the sea level. From the top, which is reached by an electric lift every few minutes, an unrivalled view is to be had of the Welsh mountains, the estuary of the Mersey, and a panorama of the adjacent country. The grounds cover an area of 35 acres, and are tastefully laid out. The theatre can accommodate 3,500 people, and has the largest stage of any theatre in the kingdom, excepting Drury Garden. Two performances are given daily during the season, and the best known variety artists engaged, and on Sundays classical concerts are held in the ballroom; most of the leading vocalists of the day are included in the programme, and the orchestra numbers close on 100, the programmes comprising the works of the most celebrated composers of the past and present. A Cafe-Chantant, conducted on Parisian lines, open free to visitors, is a popular feature, performances being given daily at 3pm and 8pm, no charge whatsoever being made for admission. The ballroom, with inlaid parquetry floor, built on 2,000 carriage springs, makes one of the finest dancing floors in the country. The menagerie contains a fine collection of animals, including two of the handsomest lions in Europe. The cycle track is pronounced by many professionals the best and fastest in the world.

• Two billiards saloons, containing eight tables made by Ashcroft, have been recently added.

• The Himalaya electric railway, water chute, and old English fair grounds, add materially to the numerous other attractions to this charming holiday resort; whilst during the season are held band concerts, eisteddfods, musical festivals, carnivals, and athletic sports, and seldom does a week pass without some special attraction being provided for the visitors.

Luncheons, dinners and teas are served at moderate charges, and the choicest brands of all kinds of liquors are supplied in various parts of the grounds.

Guide to the District of Wallasey 1902

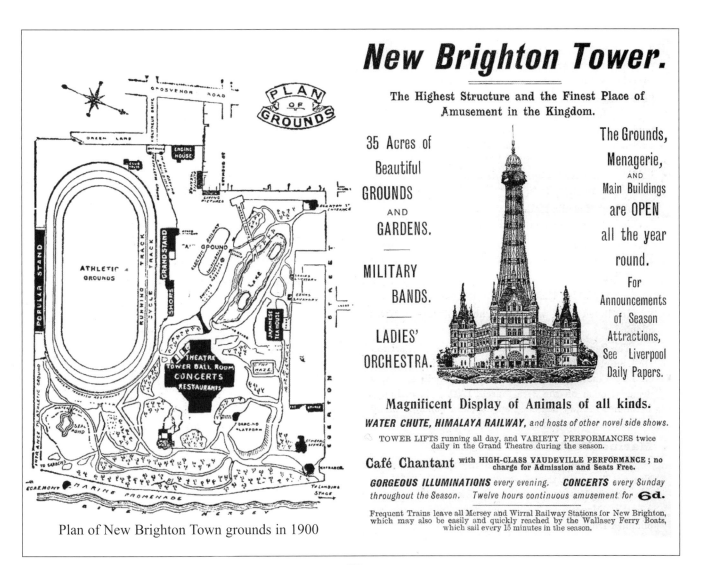

Plan of New Brighton Town grounds in 1900

—	Hurst's Bakery founded in Claughton Road **Birkenhead** [still in business today]
—	Mount Road water pumping station opened, **Tranmere**[KD]
—	**Raby Village** school closed- children accommodated at **Thornton Hough**[YW8]
—	Upton Cricket Club founded[YW7]
1 Jan	Victoria Central Hospital opened in **Liscard**[MM]
14 Jan	**Birkenhead** North End Cycling Club founded
22 Jan	Queen Victoria died
4 Feb	**New Ferry** – Brandon Street **Birkenhead** Electric Tram service commenced[BET]
Mar	**Wallasey** UDC acquired Wallasey Tramway Company including:- 9 cars, 60 horses, stables & tramlines for £20,500[TBW]
11 Mar	Woodchurch Road primary school **Birkenhead** opened in temporary premises
2 April	Foundation stone laid for Welsh Presbyterian Church, Rake Lane **Wallasey**[KD]
17 May	**Tranmere** Congregational Church opened in Old Chester road[OPB]
17 May	**Wallasey** electric tramcar service commenced[BT]
17 May	United Reformed Church opened in **Tranmere**
24 June	Harrison Drive opened – New Road from **Wallasey Village** to shore[RPW]
27 June	First electric tram rails laid at junction of Church Street & King Street **Egremont**[TBW]
1 July	Wirral Railway Goods Station opened at **Seacombe**[KD]
10 July	**Birkenhead** Town Hall fire - new tower cost £15,000[WBD]
1 Aug	Victoria Park **Tranmere** (about 27 acres) opened by Mayor Ald. T Cook[KD]
31 Aug	HMS Exmouth launched at Cammell Laird, **Birkenhead**[MOI]
21 Dec	Line of Docks route opened in **Birkenhead**[BET]

Above: Officials from the Board of Trade are posing with the No 44 tram in Beaufort Road **Birkenhead** at the opening of Birkenhead Corporation Tramways Line of Docks route on 24 December 1901[BET]

Bottom right: One of the tramcars on the **New Ferry** route which opened February 1901 is pictured at Woodside **Birkenhead**. The original 13 trams were single deck due to the low railway bridge in Chester Street near Cammell Laird. However, due to demand all the original trams were converted into double-deckers by 1910 but with flat roofs due to the bridge. Although the destination board on the tram says **Port Sunlight** the terminus was in New Ferry[BET]

Below: Victoria Central Hospital in Liscard Road **Liscard** was opened 1 January 1901 with the first patients admitted by the end of the month[MM]

Population at 1901 Census

Arrowe	121	Meols, Little	1,962
Barnston	522	Moreton-cum-Lingham	597
Bebington Hr	1,540	Ness	355
Bebington Lr	8,398	Neston, Great	2,201
Bidston	465	Neston-cum-Parkgate UD	4,15
Birkenhead	110,915	Noctorum	212
Brimstage	181	Overpool	91
Bromborough	1,891	Oxton	4,579
Burton	222	Pensby	48
Caldy	202	Poulton-cum-Seacombe	20,749
Capenhurst	159	Poulton-cum-Spital	487
Childer Thornton	685	Prenton	412
Claughton-cum-Grange	3,920	Puddington	126
Eastham	913	Raby	350
Frankby	248	Saughall Massie	186
Gayton	180	Shotwick	82
Grange	299	Storeton	263
Greasby	290	Sutton, Great	397
Heswall-cum-Oldfield	2,167	Sutton, Little	1,109
Hoose	2,701	Thingwall	156
Hooton	200	Thornton Hough	547
Hoylake & West Kirby UD	10,905	Thurstaston	141
Irby	146	Tranmere	37,709
Landican	71	Upton	788
Ledsham	82	Wallasey	4,169
Leighton	728	West Kirby	4,542
Liscard	16,323	Whitby	4,082
Meols, Great	456	Willaston	597
		Woodchurch	140

—	**Hoylake** Civic Hall opened
—	**Birkenhead** Corporation Act 1902 passed authorising the corporation to acquire Hamilton Square Gardens [KD]
—	Slatey Road Branch Police Station opened **Birkenhead**[WBD]
—	Price Street Branch Police Station opened **Birkenhead**[WBD]
—	**Liscard** Castle (Marsden's Castle or Marsden's Folly) demolished[OMW]
—	Brown Cow Vaults, Bromborough Road **Bebington** purchased by Birkenhead Brewery[YW8]
—	Navy League Home opened at **New Brighton** by Lord Strathcona[KD]
—	North & South Wales Bank, later to become Midland Bank, opened at Charing Cross **Birkenhead** (*see picture below*)
—	Open Golf championship held at Royal Liverpool Golf Club, **Hoylake**[RLGC]
—	**Heswall** Golf Club founded
—	Victoria hall **New Brighton** acquired as a Parish Hall[KD]
—	**Wallasey** Yeomanry return from Boer War[KD]
2 Mar	**Oxton & Claughton** Circle tram route opened[BET]
17 Mar	Rake Lane tram service commenced at **Wallasey**
1 Jun	Boer War – peace declared[WON]
9 Aug	Coronation of Edward VII[WON]
10 Sept	Diamond Jubilee of the Wirral & **Birkenhead** Agricultural Society at a new permanent show ground at **Bebington**[YW8]
20 Oct	**Heswall** Consumption Hospital opened[YW6]
13 Dec	**Seacombe** Promenade Recreation Ground opened

Above: These bathing huts were pictured on a postcard from **New Brighton** in 1902

Below: Liscard Castle (Marsden's Castle or Marsden's Folly) which stood at the Hoseside Road end of Seaview Road, **Wallasey** was demolished in c.1902[OMW]

Looking from Charing Cross down Grange Road **Birkenhead** in the early years of the 20th Century, the branch of the North & South Wales Bank (later to become the Midland Bank) which opened in 1902 is seen on the right. Opposite is the Birkenhead Brewery's pub *The Grange Hotel,* which has more recently been demolished and MacDonalds fast food outlet built on the site[YW2]

"The Wallasey News"

WEDNESDAY and SATURDAY.

ESSENTIALLY THE LOCAL PAPER READ BY ALL.

Contains full Reports of all Local Meetings. The Recognised Advertising Paper for all Official, Auction, Legal and Business Announcements.

Office : 55 VICTORIA ROAD, SEACOMBE,

Where Printing Orders are received and executed expeditiously and in first-class style.

All four adverts on this page were taken from *Guide to the District of Wallasey* 1902

Above: *Wallasey News* whose first issue appeared on 3 November 1899

Right: The Wallasey Grammar school advert confirms that the school was founded in the 16th century. It moved to the Withens Lane site in 1876 where it remained until 1967

Below right: Mackie & Gladstone, Wine & Spirit Merchant, Ale & Porter Bottlers and a mineral water factory, based in Birkenhead, was founded in 1836. By 1902 it had six branches and five agents. It was acquired by Birkenhead Brewery in 1948

Below left: *Hotel Victoria,* Lower Heswall was opened in 1902, taking its licence from the *White Lion* which was on the corner of Wallrake and Gayton Road

---

WALLASEY GRAMMAR SCHOOL,

WITHENS LANE, LISCARD.

FOUNDED IN THE SIXTEENTH CENTURY.

HEAD MASTER :—ALBERT J. MEAD, B.A., Lond.

Some time Senior Latin and English Master, Middle School. Liverpool College.

Second Master—W. CHAPPLE, B.A., A.K.C. Lond.

Assistant Masters—R. A. FOULKES. B.A., London ; S. ANDRADE, B.A., B.Sc., late scholar of Catharine College, Cambridge ; J. A. RADLEY, B.A., Keble College, Oxford ; A. E. FARLEY, Trin. Coll., Dublin ; W. A. KYNASTON, University of London.

SCIENCE:—*Senior Master*—S. ANDRADE, B.A., Cambridge, and B.A., B.Sc., London, and W. T. WALKER, Royal Coll. of Science, London.

FRENCH—Mons. J. BAZIN, Officier de l'instruction publique.

GERMAN—Herr OTTO C. WICKERT, University of Heidelberg.

MUSIC—J. FRED. SWIFT.

DRAWING—WILLIAM MORTON, Certificated Art Master, Royal College of Art, London.

DRILLING INSTRUCTOR—Sergt.-Major C. D. GRIFFIN, 1st C. and C.V.A.

INSTRUCTION IN CARPENTRY—JAS. SAMUEL, Certificated, City and Guilds of London Institute.

CLERK TO THE GOVERNORS—SYDNEY S. DAWSON, Chartered Accountant, 35 Dale Street, Liverpool.

FOR DAY BOYS AND BOARDERS.

The School supplies, at moderate inclusive fees, a sound education fitting for entrance to the Professions and for Commercial life. Commodious Modern Buildings (1876 and 1884)—Separate Class Rooms—*Preparatory Department quite distinct*. Special arrangements made for delicate or backward Boys—Science Lecture Room with fully-equipped Chemical Laboratory adjoining, specially built Carpenter's Shop and Physic's Laboratory.—Playing Fields (8 acres), &c.

HESWALL-ON-THE-DEE,

CHESHIRE.

HOTEL VICTORIA.

THE best-appointed Hotel in Cheshire, commanding one of the finest views of the Estuary of the Dee, combined with a magnificent and uninterrupted view of Welsh Mountain Scenery, even to the summit of Snowdon.

As a Residential Hotel it is unequalled. Strongly recommended by the medical faculty, especially for consumptives, being sheltered from the North and East winds by the Heswall hills.

Replete with every comfort. Close to Hoylake Golf Links.

————o————

Boarding Terms from Three Guineas per week.

Apply to—

MANAGERESS.

Telephone No. 21.

————o————

Heswall is within easy distance of Liverpool, Chester, and all large centres served by the L. & N.-W., Great Western, Mersey and Wirral Railways, and other means of communication.

WEEK-END TARIFF A SPECIALITY.

MACKIE & GLADSTONE,

Wine & Spirit Merchants,

ALE & PORTER BOTTLERS,

86, 88 & 90 HAMILTON STREET,

BIRKENHEAD.

BRANCHES—Bedford Road, Rock Ferry ; Church Road, Tranmere ; King Street, Egremont ; Belmont Road, New Brighton ; Market Street, Hoylake ; and Grange Road, West Kirby.

AGENTS—ALBERT GRIFFITHS, Rock Stores, Heswall ; JOHN McBRYDE, Grange Mount, Birkenhead ; J. H. STOREY, 49 Borough Road, Birkenhead ; SHAW BROS., 120 & 122 Seabank Road, Egremont ; JOHN WAYMAN, Eaton Road, West Kirby.

Mineral Water Factory: Market St., Birkenhead.

EVERY DESCRIPTION OF

WINES & SPIRITS OF THE FINEST QUALITY.

GUINNESS'S EXTRA STOUT,

AND

BASS'S, ALLSOP'S & WORTHINGTON'S ALES,

In Cask and Bottles, in Fine Condition.

MINERAL WATERS—M. & G.'s Own Manufacture. Extra quality at exceptionally low prices.

PRICE LISTS ON APPLICATION.

TELEPHONE—93 Birkenhead.   Telegrams—"MACKIE, BIRKENHEAD."

— Special Council School opened in Claughton Road **Birkenhead**[WBD]

— Birkenhead Corporation extend electricity supply to **Prenton** and **Upton**[WBD]

— Conway Street School opened in **Birkenhead**[OPB]

— **Birkenhead** shipbuilding firm Lairds amalgamated with the Sheffield company Cammell to form Cammell Laird & Co Ltd[OPB]

— English Presbyterian Church opened in Martins Lane **Wallasey**[KD]

— Hamilton Square Gardens acquired by **Birkenhead** Corporation[WBD]

— WW Kelly, an American, took over the Theatre Royal in Argyle Street **Birkenhead**

— Tender accepted to build Manor Road Schools **Wallasey** (£19,755)[KD]

— Tutteys Stores opened in Oxton Road, **Birkenhead** – operating here until 1937 when Rostances took over

— The **Birkenhead** shipbuilder Laird Bros amalgamated with the Sheffield-based steel manufacturer Charles Cammell and became Cammell Laird Ltd Shipbuilders[MOI]

13 Feb Charles Thompson, founder of the mission in **Birkenhead** died[KD]

19 Mar Birkenhead Unitarian Church, Besborough Road **Birkenhead** opened

27 Mar **Seacombe** Library opened[KD]

1 May **Wallasey** UDC became responsible as Local Education Authority for Elementary Education[KD]

3 May First electric train through the Mersey Tunnel from Liverpool to **Birkenhead**[RSW]

Jun Queen Victoria Memorial tablet unveiled at St Mary's Church **Liscard**[KD]

15 Jun New wing of Wirral & **Birkenhead** Children's Hospital opened. Cost £3,500

23 July HM cruiser *Topaze* launched at Cammell Laird **Birkenhead** [see photo next page]

Oct Gorsehill No.1 Reservoir **New Brighton** water supply from Lake Vwrnwy turned on[WON]

Built in Londonderry, the *TSS Bidston* was launched in 1903 and was put into service on the Triangular ferry service between **Rock Ferry/New Ferry** & Liverpool. This service first operated from 30 June 1899. The ship's name was later changed to the *Old Bidston* (as seen here) and in 1933 was sold to the Blackpool Passenger Steamship Co Ltd and she was renamed the *Minden*[WCS]

Below: These poor children, some without shoes, are posing for the photographer on the steps of the Charles Thompson Mission, Hemingford Street **Birkenhead**. This and similar photographs were used for publicity purposes to highlight the plight of these children and to raise funds to help feed and clothe them. The founder, Charles Thompson, died 13 February 1903 and his daughter Miss Annie Thompson continued the good work for over 60 years. She was awarded the MBE in 1953 and died in 1965. In 1968, the mission was incorporated into the Liverpool City Mission and still continues its good work today

Above: This photograph of the Mostyn House School Rifle Team was taken by Arthur Maycock of **Parkgate** on 27 July 1903. Note the boys are wearing boaters with the school crest; three masters are standing behind. They would use the sands at Parkgate for target practice

Right: The paddle steamer *Cheshire* was built at the Canada Works E & S Co Ltd **Birkenhead** in 1889 for the Birkenhead Corporation. Pictured here in 1903, she was sold to the Great Western Railway in 1905 and became a tender at Plymouth until wrecked in 1913[wcs]

Below: *HMS Topaze* passing New Brighton Tower and pier. This cruiser, which was built at Cammell Laird, was launched 23 July 1903 and completed in 1904. Built at this time she was one of a few ships that formed a link between the older cruisers and the 'modern' light cruisers. She survived action in the First World War and was sold in 1921

—	Laird Street Infants School opened **Birkenhead**[WBD]
—	Wesleyan Church opened Market Street **Hoylake** [St Lukes]
—	Grange Vale **Birkenhead** major sewer road works carried out
—	New Wesleyan Church **Liscard** opened[KD]
7 May	**Wallasey** Boer War memorial in Central Park dedicated[KD]
8 June	**Port Sunlight** Church opened by Mr Lever[CPH]
July	St Colomba Church **Egremont** consecrated[KD]
19 July	Royal Yacht Victoria & Albert which was moored off **Rock Ferry** sailed from Mersey after King Edward V11 had laid the Liverpool Anglican Cathedral foundation stone
5 Sept	Woodchurch Road primary school **Birkenhead** transfered to new building
16 Dec	**Hoylake** Institute opened in Market Street

Girls from the Claughton Higher Grade School are posing for the photographer during a cookery lesson in 1903

Christ Church **Port Sunlight** Church which was opened by Mr Wm. H Lever 8 June 1904 was built at his own expense and designed by William & Segar Owen; it was nondenominational[CPH]

Right: The **Wallasey** Boer War Memorial was unveiled in Central Park, Liscard, 7 May 1904. The inscription reads:[KD]

> Erected To The Memory
> Of The
> **WALLASEY MEN**
> Who Lost Their Lives In The
> South African War 1899–1902
> And Also In Recognition Of The Services Of
> Local Men During The Campaign

Left: The Royal Yacht *Victoria & Albert* is pictured in the River Mersey moored off **Rock Ferry** when King Edward V11 visited **Liverpool** on 19 July 1904 to lay the foundation stone for the Anglican Cathedral

Bottom Left: This picturesque and peaceful scene of **Irby** Village, taken in 1904, depicts the only shop which was also the Post Office. It was run by Mrs SE Leech whose husband, Horatio, supplemented their income with his jobs as a joiner, wheelwright and undertaker. The building in the distance is a side view of the outbuildings to Rookery Farm. There were two pubs, the Anchor Inn and *The Prince of Wales,* the nearest station was **Thurstaston** over two miles away and the population of Irby at that time was only 150

Left: One of the **Heswall Golf Club** members is driving off in front of the new clubhouse which was built in 1904. Heswall Golf Club was founded in 1902 and initially the outbuildings at Leighton Hall Farm were used as the clubhouse. It is obvious that one of the hazards in those early days were sheep! This clubhouse was burnt down in 1924 and replaced in 1926[YW6]

— The drinking fountain in the centre of **Bebington** Village moved into Mayer Park (see opposite)[YW8]

— Higher Elementary & Secondary Schools opened **Birkenhead**[WBD]

— Woodchurch Road Council School **Birkenhead** opened[WBD]

— Woodlands Council School opened[WBD]

— Mersey Park Council School **Hr Tranmere** opened[WBD]

— Laird Street Presbyterian Church opened[OPB]

— **Birkenhead** High School moved to new premises in Devonshire Place **Oxton** from Village Road

— Council plan to demolish Ham & Egg Parade **New Brighton** and construct the new Promenade and a Marine Lake[KD]

— King Flour Mills Ltd, Lower Mersey Street **Ellesmere Port** built[EP]

— New smithy at **Thornton Hough** opened

— Storeton Quarries tramway closed[ST]

Feb   Gorsehill No2 Reservoir and Water Tower opened in **New Brighton**. Combined storage capacity of the two reservoirs now 6,300,000 gallons[KD]

2 May   Manor Road Council School opened in **Wallasey**[WCLG]

29 May   Houdini appeared at the Argyle Theatre **Birkenhead**

26 Oct   Queen Eleanor Cross Hamilton Square **Birkenhead** unveiled

This postcard of **Hoylake** Lower Lighthouse was posted in 1905. The lighthouse last shone in 1908 and was demolished in December 1922

Below: Leasowe was a popular site for camping with the tents sited in front of Leasowe Lighthouse. It was not only popular with the general public but also the military in the form of the territorials who also used this area. However, the pond in the foreground is an indication that this was a low lying area and prone to flooding

The drinking fountain with signpost and street lamp above, pictured in the centre of **Bebington** Village, was a gift of Charles Hill in 1863. In 1905, due to a road widening scheme it was moved to a site in Mayer Park. Note the bollards around the monument to stop horse-drawn vehicles from crashing into and damaging it. Recently the fountain has been moved back into Bebington Village[YW8]

Argyle Theatre
BIRKENHEAD.
Manager -   - D. J. CLARKE.

Two Performances Nightly, at 6-50 & 9.
MATINEE every Thursday at 2-30.

MONDAY, May 29th, 1905,

HOUDINI

WEE MONA
BOSTON TWINS
J. W. RIGBY
ANNIE MYERS
LILY RAMSDALE
CHAS. AUSTIN

THE BREWSTERS

The Orchestra under the direction of
Mr. E. DENNEY.

POPULAR PRICES.

This Advertisement for the Argyle Theatre **Birkenhead** 29 May 1905 included among the artists the world famous Houdini

The Wirral Harriers are seen meeting in front of the *Old Red Lion* **Little Sutton.** This pub dated back to at least 1850 when Mary Tyrer was the victualler. This old building was demolished in 1934 and the licence transfered to the new *Ye Old Red Lion* pub, to the right of and at right angles to the one pictured. The Chester Road was widened and now runs through the site of this this old public house

Pictured on the beach at **Hoylake** in this postcard sent in 1906

— Woodchurch Road Welsh Methodist Church opened in **Birkenhead**[OPB]

— **Hoylake** Congregational Chapel built[WBD]

— Park Road & Cleveland Street temporary schools opened in **Birkenhead**[WBD]

— Girl's secondary school opened in Conway Street   transferred to new building in Park Road South **Birkenhead** in 1928

— GPO opened in Argyle Street **Birkenhead**[KD]

— **Wallasey** ferry boats *SS Iris & Daffodil* were built

— **New Brighton's** infamous Ham & Egg Parade was purchased by **Wallasey** Corporation for demolition[KD]

— Work started on the promenade extension - **New Brighton** Pier to West boundary of Marine Park

— Oakdale Presbyterian Church Hall opened in **Wallasey Village**[KD]

— **Seacombe** Methodist School foundation stone laid[KD]

1 Jan   Mr WH Lever elected Liberal MP for Wirral[KD]

6 Feb   *SS Fearless* collided with coasting vessel and was beached, then split in half, off **New Brighton**

11 April Foundation stone laid for St Georges Congregational Church at **Thornton Hough**[YW8]

12 April Japanese battleship arrived in **Birkenhead**[YW2]

5 Dec   Highfield Bowling Club founded at **Rock Ferry**

12 Dec **Wallasey Village** Parish church hall opened[KD]

Above: The Japanese warship *Katori*, which was built at Vickers Barrow in 1906, paying a visit to **Birkenhead** 12 April. The crew visited Lever Bros. at Port Sunlight[YW2]

The Lower Parade **New Brighton** is seen to the right of the Ham & Egg Parade pictured opposite The area seen in front of *The Palace* was to change within a year when the promenade was widened and extended to Waterloo Road. *The Palace* amusement arcade also had the largest plunge baths in the country and it was here that the largest Big Wheel in the country was planned in 1896 but this never happened. There are still indoor amusements on the site today

Below: The Cammell Laird Ambulance Corps are posing behind one of their stretchers on wheels, complete with canopy, for the photographer A Morris of **Birkenhead** in May 1906. The only person not named at the bottom of the picture is the dog!

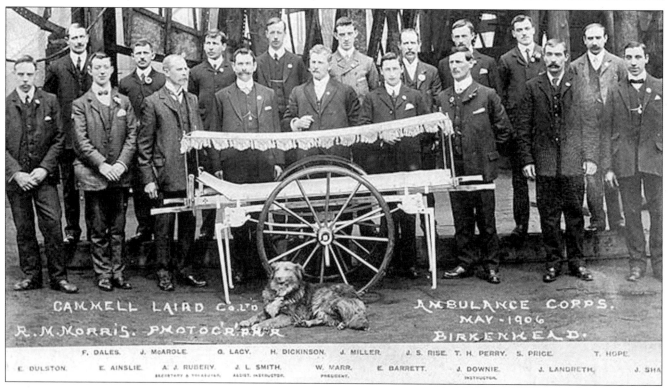

This view off **New Brighton** is not of two ships but of the *SS Fearless* which after colliding with a coasting vessel was beached and then split in half on 6 February 1906. She was eventually broken up on Tranmere Foreshore

Above: The infamous Ham & Egg Parade (otherwise known as Aquarium Parade or Teapot Row) is viewed from the shadows of **New Brighton** Pier. This four-storied building was built on two levels with the lower level containing the notorious shops and so-called tearooms where shop keepers would accost passers by. Following a local referendum on 27 January 1906 the Wallasey Corporation purchased the parade properties and demolished them

Below: Banks Road **West Kirby** is pictured in 1906 with Dee Lane in the distance and The Crescent off to the right of the Cafe sign. Further to the right are the single storey shops of Quellyn Robert's Wine & Spirits store at No 3 (renumbered No 7) and John Taylor's Confectionery next door which is now Lingham's Bookshop. These shops were built in the garden of the first house and others have subsequently been built in the gardens of the houses on the right

—	**Bidston** Hill dedicated as an open space[OPB]
—	Mersey Park Junior Mixed and Infants School opened in **Hr Tranmere**[OPB]
—	Dr Crippen, later to become the infamous murderer, gave a medical lecture at the Assembly Rooms, Albion Street, **New Brighton**[MMM]
—	Leasowe Road Station (later **Wallasey Village**) opened[RSW]
—	**New Brighton** Tower grounds attraction for the season was an Abyssinian Village[WON]
—	Open Golf championship held at Royal Liverpool Golf Club, **Hoylake**. Won by a Frenchman Arnaud Massy, who named his newly born daughter Hoylake![RLGC]
—	**Poulton** officially separated from the mother parish of **Wallasey**[KD]
1 Jan	Mr WH Lever elected MP for Wirral
9 Mar	St George's Road Elementary school opened by **Wallasey** Council[WON]
16 Mar	**New Brighton** Ferry landing stage torn from its moorings in a gale and floated down the Mersey *(see below)*

9 Apr	Margaret Ismay of *Dawpool,* **Thurstaston,** wife of Thomas, died[Th]
16 Apr	Foundation stone laid for new **Egremont** Presbyterian Church[KD]
May	Ham & Egg Parade property, **New Brighton,** which had been purchased by local corporation in 1905 for £41,000 was demolished
4 May	Highfield Bowling Club opened in Highfield Road, **Rock Ferry**
29 May	St Georges Congregational Church at **Thornton Hough** dedicated (see opposite)[YW8]
22 Jun	Work completed on the promenade extension at **New Brighton** from the Pier to West boundary of Marine Park and the commemoration stone was laid by Mr WH Lever MP[KD]
16 July	New Cunard liner *Lusitania* arrived in the Mersey
Oct	Winter Gardens, **New Brighton** opened[KD]
1 Nov	**Caldy** Parish Church, Church of the Resurrection and All Saints, opened[YW3]

Right: Members of the Wirral Archers photographed in **Birkenhead** Park in 1907. From the left John Keyworth; Osmond Alan Keyworth (his son) and Margaret Keyworth (his wife)

Below: The two bridges of **New Brighton** pier which connected it to the Ferry landing stage are seen in the river following a fierce westerly gale 16 March 1907. The stage was torn from its moorings and floated down the Mersey, later to be towed back[WON]

The original **Eastham** Ferry Hotel's trade was from the ferry crossing to Liverpool which proved very lucrative. However, most of this trade was taken away when the Chester to Birkenhead Railway opened in 1840, providing a much quicker and less hazardous journey across the Mersey. A new Eastham Ferry Hotel, pictured on the right in 1907, was erected in 1846 to encourage new visitors to Eastham either by coach or ferry.

One of the more visible attractions was the Jubilee Arch which is pictured on the left. This ornate structure was erected in London Road for Queen Victoria's visit to Liverpool in her Jubilee year of 1897 and later moved to Eastham. This was the entrance to Eastham Ferry Gardens and the sign on the left indicates the entrance price of 2d [1p]. This price covered entertainments inside which included a looping-the-loop ride which could reach an estimated speed of 95mph but proved too scary for the public, Fred Brook's Vaudeville & Circus Co., pierrot theatre, ballroom, bear pit, menagerie, zoological gardens, sideshows and tea rooms[YW9]

This photograph of St George's Congregational Church at **Thornton Hough** being built by Smith Bros. of Burnley was taken 18 July 1906 – between laying the foundation stone on 11 April 1906 and the dedication 29 May 1907. It was built for Wm Hesketh Lever on the site of several plain cottages and a smithy. He replaced the cottages with attractively designed ones and built the present smithy at the entrance to the village also planting the chestnut tree in front[YW8]

— **Prenton** Road West Congregational Church built[OPB]

— Extension to **Bidston** Hill recreation ground[WBD]

— New North Branch Library opened in **Birkenhead**[WBD]

— New Post Office building opened Argyle Street **Birkenhead**[WBD]

— Presbyterian Church Manor Road **Wallasey** opened

— Council School opened at **Poulton**[KD]

— **Egremont** Pier extension cost £13,310[KD]

— Extension of Central Park **Liscard** (cost £8,220)[KD]

— **New Brighton** Golf Links purchased by Wallasey Corporation £15,500[KD]

— Oakdale Recreation Ground **Seacombe** laid out at a cost of £1,325[KD]

— Gift of £9,000 received from Mr Carnegie for the erection of Earlston Library **Wallasey**[KD]

— **Wallasey** Council opened Vaughan Road Elementary School[KD]

24 Jan   Boy Scout movement inaugurated at **Birkenhead** YMCA in Grange Road[SS]

7 Apr   Guinea Gap sea water baths opened at **Seacombe**[KD]

25 Apr   **Tranmere** Rovers become Combination Champions[TR]

14 July   Lower Lighthouse **Hoylake** last lit, then became the entrance to the Lighthouse Pavilion Theatre[HMP]

15 July   **Leasowe** Lighthouse ceased to operate. Opened up later as tea rooms[YW5]

16 July   Higher Elementary School officially opened at **New Brighton**[KD]

30 July   **Wallasey** Central Liberal Club opened[WON]

22 Aug   **Liscard Village** branch of Liverpool Bank opened[WON]

5 Sept   Women's Suffrage demonstration at St George's Hall which included the **Birkenhead** & Wirral Branch *(see opposite)*

Below: The Wallasey Lancashire Fortress Engineers (WLFE) who were based at *HMS Annettin* in Clarence Dock, are seen at their 15 day camp held at the Warren **New Brighton**. Many of the men were employees of Wallasey Ferries. Originally named the Mersey Division Royal Engineers Submarine Miners who were responsible for the defence of the Mersey by laying mines

The **Birkenhead** and Wirral Suffragettes are seen with their banner on St Georges Plateau, Liverpool 5 September 1908. The timing of this display was to coincide with the Chancellor Lloyd George speaking at a Liberal Rally at Sun Hall, Kensington, Liverpool. Having suffered disruption from suffragettes elsewhere, he insisted that no women were to be allowed at the meeting and this was agreed to. However, four women wearing sashes of the Women's Social and Political Union (WSPU) drove to and fro in front of the hall, delivering short speeches by megaphone to a large cheering crowd. This resulted in two of them being arrested and held at Prescot Street Police Station until the meeting was over.

One of their supporters was Arthur Bulley, a prosperous Liverpool cottonbroker who founded Ness Gardens. He stood as Labour Parliamentary Candidate for Rossendale using women' suffrage as part of his campaign which he lost, but perhaps not because of his suffrage beliefs

Girls are seen 'plaiting the maypole' at the Neston May Queen Festival of 1908

Prenton Golf Club's new club house, which was opened in 1908, is pictured above. The two famous amateurs from Royal Liverpool Golf Club, John Ball & John Graham, took part in an exhibition game. The club had been formed 18 February 1905 using land extending from what is now Elm Road onto the Waterworks track, now Waterpark Road. The membership grew so quickly that by December of 1905 a temporary ground was ready for play on part of which is the present course. The new course was officially opened 6 April 1906 with the original, temporary club house pictured on the left, being used for other purposes.

Above: The children, who are dressed up for the Oddfellows Club at **Childer Thornton** 7 July 1908, are passing in front of the *Halfway House* at Childer Thornton
Below: Crowds are gathered at the poolside of Guinea Gap Baths for the opening on 7 April 1908 by Mr TV Burrows, Chairman of the Health Committee. These were **Wallasey's** first municipal baths which were built at a cost of £15,000. The murky water is due to the fact that at that time sea water was pumped direct from the River Mersey into the baths!

Prior to the promenade being built at **Seacombe** there was a breach in the river wall known as Guinea Gap (named after golden guineas found there C.1850). This was a safe place to swim as it was free from dangerous currents

The YMCA building Grange Road **Birkenhead**, is pictured on the right. It was opened in 1890 but will be remembered for being the venue on 25 January 1908 for Baden-Powell's inaugural speech for the founding of the Boy Scout movement. The plaque which commemorated the event is now situated at the present YMCA building in Whetstone Lane. Because of this link with the Boy Scouts, the Borough was asked to host the International Jamboree on the 21st anniversary which was held at Arrowe Park in 1929[ss]

—	Extensive damage caused to St James Church **New Brighton,** especially the organ, after a gas explosion which also damage local houses
—	St Matthews C of E Church Park Road East built **Birkenhead**[WBD]
—	New South Branch Library opened **Birkenhead**[WBD]
—	Christ Church Baptist Mission Chapel opened near the Wirral Colliery **Little Neston** for the use of the colliers and their families.
—	4th Battalion Cheshire Regiment spent summer camp at Abergaveny
—	Emmanuel Church **Liscard** completed[KD]
—	Extension of Tramways to **Wallasey Village** commenced (cost £83,160)[TBW]
—	First official Scout camp ever was held at Dodd's Farm **Irby**[YW6]
—	Foundation Stone of **New Brighton** presbyterian Church laid[KD]
—	Quarry between Rake Lane and Withens Lane **Wallasey** purchased as an open space[KD]
—	St Luke's Church **Poulton** raised £1,000 by bazaar[KD]
—	St Stephen's Church **Prenton** completed[OPB]
—	**Wallasey** High School for Girls opened in Mount Pleasant Road (see photographs)[WON]
—	**Wallasey** Wesleyan Church Foundation Stone laid[KD]
12 Feb	Dominion liner Ottoman crashed into **Seacombe** landing stage

6 Mar	Vittoria Dock disaster **Birkenhead**. 14 workmen were killed when a high spring tide and strong winds caused the coffer dam to collapse. [YW7]
15 April	Opening service for newly built **Heswall** Presbyterian Church of England Telegraph Road
May	**Caldy** railway station opened[RSW]
May	Princess Louise and the Duke of Argyle visited the Navy League Homes Withens Lane **Wallasey**[WON]
5 June	New Catholic school of St Albans opened in Mill Lane **Wallasey** opened[KD]
15 June	New covered extension to **Birkenhead** Market opened[YW2]
15 July	**Hoylake** Cottage Hospital foundation stone laid
21 Aug	The *Gaelic* went ashore at **Egremont**, *(see photo)*
Sept	**Wallasey** municipal golf course opened in Harrison Park[KD]
3 Sept	*Akbar* nautical school opened at Heswall *(see photograph below)*[YW1]
19 Oct	New **Birkenhead** Central Library opened in Market Street South[WBD]
19 Oct	**Wallasey** Earlston Central Library opened
31 Oct	All Saints' Church (temporary Church building) opened in Hoseside Road **Wallasey**[WON]
15 Nov	**Wallasey Village** branch of the Bank of Liverpool opened[WON]
Dec	**Hoylake** Parade Higher Elementary School opened[OPB]

Left: Children are enjoying model yachting at Central Park **Liscard**

Below: The *Akbar* nautical training school opened at **Heswall** 3 August 1909 in ten acres of ground at a cost of over £17,000. It was built for the Juvenile Reform Committee who had previously used training ships moored off Tranmere, but an ageing ship with rotten timbers had convinced them to build a more permanent shore station. The nautical school, which was organised on Navy standards, was best known locally for its band which appeared at most of the local events.

It was one of eight training schools to be shut down when it finally closed 16 February 1956[YW1]

Wallasey High School was established in the Concert Hall in Manor Road Liscard in 1883 by a private company. In 1890 the school moved further down Manor Road to a house at the corner of Stringhey Road. The school was taken over in 1906 by Cheshire County Council and in 1909 moved to the new buildings pictured above in Mount Pleasant.

The photograph below, which was taken in 1912, shows girls exercising in the school gymnasium[WHS]

The proprietor is standing proudly in the doorway of his Market Stores at 27 Poulton Road **Seacombe** together with his three staff, probably unaware that a bare-footed urchin boy is also in the photograph! The game and poultry hanging in front of the shop, although not very healthy, was a common site in those days

The *Gaelic* is pictured on its side in the River Mersey off **Egremont** 21 August 1909

— **Leasowe** Castle purchased by the Trustees of the Railway Convalescent Homes for £11,750[RPW]

— Laird Street Baptist Church opened in **Birkenhead**[OPB]

— **Birkenhead** & District Co-op central offices opened in Catherine Street[YW7] Methodist Church opened[KD]

— **Egremont** Presbyterian Church – new Hall opened and memorial windows unveiled[KD]

— **Hoylake** Cottage Hospital opened

— Mr Gersham Stewart returned MP for Wirral

— **Wallasey** Golf Links opened on the site of the former New Brighton Golf Club which had been purchased by Wallasey Council for £15,000 in 1909[YW5]

1 Jan **Birkenhead** Brewery introduced milk stout

26 April Foundation stone laid for St Nicholas' Church, **Wallasey**[WON]

6 May King Edward V11 died[WON]

25 May Wesleyan Church opened in Claremount Road **Wallasey**[WON]

7 July **New Brighto**n Presbyterian Church opened[WON]

8 July St Luke's Church, Wallasey opened[WON]

8 July Wallasey Tramway extended to **Poulton**[TBW]

19 July Royal Charter granted to **Wallasey**[WON]

Oct Mrs Pankhurst addressed an audience on The *Suffragette Movement* at the assembly rooms, Albion Street **New Brighton**[YW4]

9 Nov The election for **Wallasey's** first Municipal Council when the Liberals were returned and Mr JT Chester was chosen as first Mayor[KD]

29 Nov First passenger flight across the River Mersey, in a bi-plane, by Mr CC Paterson and Mr RA King, landing on the Royal Liverpool Golf Course, **Hoylake**[YW3]

Three **Heswall** Churches proposed a joint protest to the Chief Constable of Cheshire against the dust nusiance caused by motor traffic along Telegraph Road while the Christian congregations of Heswall were going to and from their respective places of worship!

The foundation stone for the Harrison Memorial (St Nicholas) Church **Wallasey Village** was laid in Harrison Drive 26 April 1910. It was built for the Harrison family in memory of their well known father & mother – James & Jane Harrison at a cost of £15.000. Built of Storeton stone by J Thomas & Sons of Oxton it was consecrated 29 November 1911[WON]

Above: This postcard, taken by J George Davies of Port Sunlight on 1 August 1910, shows children celebrating the Hr **Bebington** Church Anniversary with the girl holding a cushion in her hand about to crown the queen who is sitting down

Right: According to the message on the back of this postcard, this view of the Town Hall in Church Street, **Seacombe** shows the public offices decorated following the death of King Edward VII who died on 6 May 1910

Tutty's Stores on the right at Nos 17-21 Oxton Road **Birkenhead** started trading here from 1904 until 1937 when Rostances took over until they closed down in 1977. The *Grange Hotel* at Charing Cross can be seen in the background.

The two children are staring in wonder at the dog sitting on the pony's back while the 'circus' girl, who is lying on the sand with a horse and her foal, is posing for the photographer – Wilkinson of New Brighton. This picture postcard, which was posted in 1910, was taken at **New Brighton,** the group were probably performing at either New Brighton Tower Grounds or at the Tower Circus[YW4]

—	**Birkenhead** Art Gallery & Museum opened in Hamilton Street[WBD]
—	Foundation stone laid for Alwen Reservoir, which was to supply water to **Birkenhead**
—	Building commenced on the King Edward VII Memorial Clock erected in Argyle Street, **Birkenhead**[BPH]
—	Lighthouse Pavilion **Hoylake** opened
—	New Baptist Church opened at **New Brighton**[KD]
—	**New Brighton** Promenade extension completed[KD]
—	Recreation Ground at BelvidereRoad, **Wallasey,** purchased[KD]
—	Whetstone Lane Fire Station extended in **Birkenhead**[WBD]
Jan	Baden Powell Girl Guides - 1st **Birkenhead** West formed[TW]
Jan	Parish of All Saints & St Bedes **Birkenhead** formed
13 Jan	**Wallasey's** first Civic Ball held in New Brighton Tower Ballroom[WON]
14 Jan	**Wallasey** Grammar School's new buildings opened[WON]
7 Feb	**Poulton** tram route to Grove Road **Wallasey Village** opened[TBW]
18 Mar	New Drill Hall at **Seacombe** opened[WON]
9 May	Foundation stone laid for **Wallasey** Masonic Hall in Manor Road[WON]
20 May	Baptist Church Seabank Road opened[WON]
12 June	**Leasowe** Castle formally opened as a Convalescent Home for Railwaymen[RPW]
22 June	Coronation of King George V – public bonfires at **Birkenhead** Park & Mersey Park **Tranmere**[KD]
July	Foundation Stone laid for new presbyterian Church in **Seacombe**[KD]
Aug	GM Schilling visited **New Brighton** where he related his many interesting exploits (See this page)
3 Sept	Jewish Synagogue opened in Falkland Road **Wallasey**[KD]
28 Sept	Auction of the estate of the late Sir Thomas Brocklebank, one of the pioneer ship-owners, at **Bebington, Storeton &Tranmere** including the quarries and Storeton Railway
30 Sept	New extension opened to Earlston Central Library, Earlston Road, **Wallasey,** opened funded by the Carnegie Trust. Mr Andrew Carnegie was an American millionaire[WON]
4 Nov	Electric Picture House opened in New Chester Road **Rock Ferry**[SSW1]
11 Nov	**Birkenhead** Masonic Hall opened in Oliver Street[WON]
25 Nov	**Liscard** Electric Picture House opened, Seaview Road[SSW2]
29 Nov	St Nicholas' Church Harrison Drive **Wallasey** consecrated[WON]

This is an advertising postcard for George M Schilling, the famous American athlete and the world's greatest walker who is pictured beside the 'Rolling Globe'. The Globe, being 7 feet in diameter and weighed 6.5 cwt, was his home in which he slept for his second attempt at walking around the world for an £8,000 wager. He stopped off at **New Brighton** in August 1911 and related his many interesting exploits to an audience at the back of Marine Park

The 'penny-in-the-slot' machines are seen at the front of Bank Cottage Farm, **Raby Mere.** In a field at the back there were swings, roundabouts etc and room for a picnic

Earlston House, Earlston Road, **Wallasey,** which was originally a private house, was purchased by the Local Board in 1898 for £20,000 and in 1899 the Central Library was opened there. In 1908 a grant of £9,000 from the Carnegie Trust was used to build an extension which was opened 30 September 1911

Population at 1911 Census	
Arrowe	111
Barnston	641
Bebington Hr	1,689
Bebington Lr	11,401
Bidston	969
Birkenhead	130,794
Brimstage	181
Bromborough	1,891
Burton	264
Caldy	183
Capenhurst	146
Childer Thornton	688
Claughton-cum-Grange	7,909
Eastham	1,084
Frankby	270
Gayton	238
Grange	445
Greasby	476
Heswall-cum-Oldfield	3,616
Hooton	226
Hoylake & West Kirby UD	11,009
Irby	161
Landican	80
Ledsham	152
Liscard	38,659
Moreton-cum-Lingham	989
Ness	451
Neston-cum-Parkgate UD	4,596
Noctorum	203
Overpool	93
Oxton	4,798
Pensby	74
Poulton-cum-Seacombe	30,566
Poulton-cum-Spital	551
Prenton	1,303
Puddington	205
Raby	351
Saughall Massie	211
Shotwick	77
Storeton	280
Sutton, Great	414
Sutton, Little	1,327
Thingwall	200
Thornton Hough	602
Thurstaston	138
Tranmere	49,257
Upton	1,006
Wallasey	9,279
Whitby	10,366
Willaston	806
Woodchurch	138

This group of morris dancers are performing at the Wallasey Club sports in **Wallasey Village** 26 June 1911

This is a group of 1st **Birkenhead** Girl Guides, formed January 1911 seen posing in Hamilton Square with the Town Hall in the background. The initial group of 12 wore dark green uniforms and always carried poles

Pictured in Hill Road, **Bidston**, this group of men are members of the Hill Road Section of the Birkenhead Special Police in 1911. They were joining up to help the authorities control what became known as the Liverpool Strike

Coronation Day festivities at **Eastham** 22 June 1911

The crowds are gathered in **Liscard** Park for a Coronation Fete 22 June 1911. Wallasey Council ordered 11,750 Coronation Mugs for the children of Wallasey from a German manufacturer. Following a local outcry they eventually chose an English Staffordshire Mug. They also gave the children a whole weeks holiday to celebrate the Coronation

—	Memorial Clock Tower to Alderman Jas Smith opened at Quarry Grounds, **New Brighton**[WON]
—	Extension to Somerville School, **Seacombe**[KD]
4 Mar	**Birkenhead** Museum & Art Gallery opened in the old library building in Hamilton Street[WBD]
30 Mar	The Arno recreation ground opened - six acre site in **Oxton**[WBD]
3 Apr	**Birkenhead** Chamber of Commerce fomally inaugurated[WBD]
12 May	**Liscard, Poulton & Seacombe** united in the township of Wallasey
14 Aug	Largest floating dock launched at Cammell Laird, **Birkenhead**[MOI]
25 Sept	**Seacombe** Presbyterian Church, new premises dedicated on the corner of Brougham Road and Church Road[WON]
Oct	Liscard Battery **New Brighton** sold to Liverpool Yacht Club for £1,600
24 Oct	King Edward V11 memorial clock unveiled in **Birkenhead**[BPH]
5 Dec	Parish Hall at **New Brighton** opened by the Bishop of Chester[KD]

New Brighton Tower is pictured in 1912 behind *The Palace* in this view from the beach. The new promenade has been built [compare with 1906 photo before the promenade]

This postcard sent to Miss Alice Joynson from her Aunt Polly was dated 7 September 1912 in the early days of aviation. The children playing on **Wallasey** sands seem oblivious to the unusual sight at that time of an aeroplane. The name RA King is seen on the aircraft canopy. It was Mr King together with a Mr Paterson that created history when they flew the first passenger flight over the Mersey 29 November 1910[YW3]

Below: In this 1912 postcard, the sign for the *Argyle Theatre* can be seen in the centre of this photograph looking down Argyle Street **Birkenhead** with Grange Road off to the left. The theatre was opened 21 December 1868 by Dennis Grannell. His nephew, Dennis Clarke, became sole manager in 1891 and it was he who was responsible for making this one of the best known theatres outside London. It received a direct hit during a bombing raid 26 September 1940 and was destroyed. Beatties' Car Park occupies part of the site today

This 1st Year Class photograph of Somerville Council School, **Seacombe** was taken on 7 June 1912. There does not seem to be any standard uniform – some boys are wearing ordinary ties and some bow ties, some wear jackets and some not. However, most boys are wearing large white collars and all the boys on the front row are wearing plus-four trousers.

This postcard of the **Birkenhead** Borough Band was sent by their Hon Treasurer John Sharp 5 October 1912

The King Edward VII Memorial Clock Tower is pictured in its original position with the pub in the background on the corner of Argyle Street and Grange Road **Birkenhead.** It was unveiled 24 October 1912 but moved to its present position *c.*1929 due to the building of the Mersey Tunnel approach roads.

The ill-fated *Titanic* sank on her maiden voyage to New York on 15 April 1912 with some 705 being saved out of a total of over 2,200 passengers and crew. She was a White Star liner whose founders, the Ismay family, had lived at *Dawpool* **Thurstaston**. The Chairman, Bruce Ismay, was one of those saved from the disaster and was never allowed to forget the fact that he survived while many women and children did not.

— **New Brighton** lifeboats had saved 524 lives in 50 years between 1863 and 1913[WON]

— Addition of Children's Ward to Victoria Central Hospital **Liscard**[KD]

— **Bidston** Lighthouse last used

— Sanction to North Mead site for **Wallasey** Town Hall. Cost for building £79,750 and road widening £1,500[KD]

— Kings Cinema opened in StationRoad **Ellesmere Port**

— Marlowe Road Congregational Church opened in **Wallasey**[KD]

— Queens Picture House opened in Whitby Road **Ellesmere Port**

— Launch of HMS *Audacious* (Super Dreadnought) Cammell Laird **Birkenhead**[MOI]

— Open Golf Championship held at Royal Liverpool Golf Club **Hoylake** – won by JH Taylor[RLGC]

31 Mar   At midnight control of local police transferred from the County to **Wallasey**[WON]

1 Apr   **Wallasey** granted County Borough status[WON]

1 Apr   **Wallasey** Police Force came into being. Head-quarters established in Manor Road **Liscard** and sub-stations opened at **Seacombe & New Brighton.** Total numbers of all ranks was 90

14 Apr   Point to Point races held at **Ledsham** [see photo]

3 May   Victoria Gardens, built on part of the site of the 'Ham & Egg Parade' **New Brighton,** opened by Lord Derby – cost £10,000. The open–air bandstand was also opened at the same time; this was later to be covered-in and became the Floral Pavilion[KD]

12 May   Cosmo Cinema opened in **Wallasey Village**[SSW2]

June **Hoylake** open-air baths opened[YW3]

Aug   Old thatched cottage opposite **Liscard** Post Office demolished[WON]

The 1913 **Wallasey** Rose Queen

Below: Some of the dignitaries are posing for a photograph while others enjoy lunch time at the Wirral Point to Point races, **Ledsham** 14 April 1913

There is plenty of hospitality.
AT BIRKENHEAD.

A pianist is playing to the audience in this photograph of the Bandstand in Victoria Gardens, **New Brighton** whch opened 3 May 1913 as an open-air summer theatre. In 1925 a glass structure enclosed the theatre and it then became the Floral Pavilion

Left: This Comic Postcard by the artist Ernest Noble depicts the new wonder of the day – aviation – in a humorous way connected with the friendliness of the people of **Birkenhead**

Below: This Carbonora & Co of Liverpool Postcard shows the Masons marching to the laying of the foundation stone of the new Masonic Hall in Oliver Street [back of Grange Road] **Birkenhead** on 13 Novemeber 1913

—	**Wallasey** Golf Club gave permission for the Liverpool District Royal Engineers to use part of the links for rifle firing practice. A red flag was to be flown at the clubhouse and on the course during shooting
25 Mar	King George V & Queen Mary visit Wirral – • Tour around Cammell Laird shipyard **Birkenhead** • Opened the public park on Bidston Hill • Laid foundation stone for **Wallasey** TownHall • Visited Lady Lever Art Gallery **Port Sunlight**[WON]
6 Apr	Tivoli Theatre **New Brighton** opened by Lily Langtree
21 July	**Leasowe** Children's Hospital opened[WON]
4 Aug	War declared **Wallasey** inaugurates Mayor's Fund for Great European War
13 Aug	Voluntary Aid Detachment formed in **Hoylake**[VS]
Aug	**Leasowe** Castle appropriated by the War Office for army purposes and later used to house German prisoners of war
19 Aug	*Birkenhead* News Prince of Wales Relief Fund inaugurated[VS]
21 Aug	Volunteer Corps formed at **Eastham**[VS]
23 Aug	Local Women Sufrage Societies abandon propoganda work and offer to help for relief and other work[VS]
24 Aug	**Bromborough** War Relief Committee formed[VS]
25 Aug	St Catherine's Hospital **Tranmere** became a Military Hospital[VS]
1 Sept	**Port Sunlight** meeting for re-formation of a Wirral Battalion of the Cheshire Regiment by Sir Henry MacKinnon[VS]
2 Sept	Mr Gersham Stewart (MP) supports big recruiting meeting at **Hoylake**[VS]
3 Sept	Recruiting meeting at **Heswall** presided over by Mr Charles MacIver, JP, CC[VS]
5 Sept	Major Strong addresses a recruiting meeting in the Haymarket, **Birkenhead**[VS]
7 Sept	700 **Port Sunlight** men depart for Chester[VS]
12 Sept	*Birkenhead* News started its Patriots' Gallery. By the end of the war over 6,000 portraits had appeared[VS]
2 Oct	Fifty-two Belgian refugees arrived at the Towers Victoria Park **Tranmere**[VS]
4 Nov	Red Cross Society open 19 Palm Grove **Oxton** as a convalescent home or temporary hospital[VS]
18 Nov	Bantams Battalion started by Mr A Bigland MP previously men under 5ft 6in were refused entry into the army[VS]
3Dec	**Rock Ferry** Council School given to 2nd Bantams Battalion[VS]
9 Dec	The 4th Cheshires leave **Birkenhead**[VS]
23 Dec	**Port Sunlight** starts Volunteer Training Corps[VS]
25 Dec	One Hundred wounded soldiers arrive at Woodside Station, **Birkenhead**[VS]

Wallasey tramcar No 54 has been decorated with bunting, flags, flowers and 2,300 light bulbs for the Royal Visit of King George V and Queen Mary on 25 March 1914. He laid the foundation stone for Wallasey's new Town Hall[TBW]

There are two centenaries to celebrate at **Neston** – Neston Ladies Day, which was founded in 1814 and Mrs Turner in the bath chair was born in that year. The society members would subscribe regularly to its fund and could claim financial assistance in times of illness, pregnancy or death. The society is still in existence and is the only one of its type to survive today[YW1]

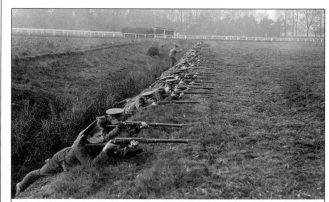

Rifle practice for the troops in trenches at **Hooton** Racecourse, the railings can be seen in the background *(see next page)*

The four photographs on this page are all connected to the outbreak of World War One 4 August 1914

Above Top: **Hooton** Park including the pictured Hooton Hall was used by the military for training purposes from 15 September

Above : This group of new recruits, all eager to be in the photograph, are pictured at **Hooton** prior to obtaining their uniform and oblivious to what lay ahead for them in the war that was expected to be over by Christmas. Many of them never returned

Below Left: This group of Lever Bros **Port Sunlight** employees are seen marching off to war following Lever Bothers 'Call to Arms' where men between 19 and 35 were encouraged to give their services to King and country with their situations being kept open for them when they returned. In all 3,206 Lever Bros employees (not including associated companies) served with the military and navy during the First World War[vs]

Below Right: As early as 8 August 1914 wounded Belgians were received in **Birkenhead** Borough Hospital

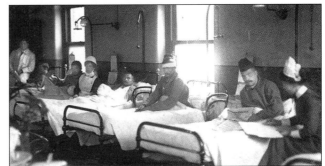

—	**Wallasey** raises a 'Nurse Cavell' Memorial Fund and places Tablet in the Victoria Central Hospital[VS]
20 Jan	Two thousand employees of Lever Bros, **Port Sunlight** now with the Colours[VS]
23 Jan	Rifle Range opened at **Hoylake**[VS]
22 Feb	Harry Lauder appeals for recruits at the **Birkenhead** Argyle Theatre[VS]
26 Feb	Wounded soldiers given an open invitation to Argyle Theatre **Birkenhead**[VS]
12 Mar	Gas worker's strike in **Birkenhead**[VS]
21 Mar	Lord Kitchener inspects **Birkenhead** Bantams at St George's Hall Liverpool[VS]
31 Mar	Hemingford Street Schools **Birkenhead** to be given to Army Council for hospital accommodation[VS]
7 May	*Lusitania* torpedoed off Ireland - many of the crew were from Merseyside
10 May	Lusitania Riots in **Birkenhead & Seacombe**[WON]
10 July	Kingsway Cinema opened in Market Street **Hoylake**[SSW2]
16 Jul	Girl Guides entertainment at St Saviour's Parish Hall **Oxton** to provide funds for water carts in France[VS]
22 Jul	Birkenhead High School **Oxton** raise funds for Victoria League Club for soldiers[VS]
Aug	Generating Station opened in Dock Road **Poulton** to supply Wallasey[WCLG]
7 Aug	Girl Guide's inspection at **Ledsham** by Sir Robert and Lady Baden Powell[VS]
13 Sept	First six girl tram conductors started duty in **Birkenhead**[TBW]
Oct	**Hoylake** Munition factory set up[VS]
23 Oct	New Fire Station at **Liscard** opened[WON]
26 Oct	*Birkenhead* News Edith Cavell Fund started[VS]
17 Nov	Robbery at **Birkenhead** Museum, Hamilton Street
4 Dec	Concert at **Port Sunlight** to aid funds of Port Sunlight Volunteers[VS]

A scheme for the **Hoylake** Munition factory was submitted in October 1915 by Mr J Crosland Graham, Mr WS Crichton, Dr J Royston and other local gentlemen. It was to be housed in an existing garage near to Hoylake Station and initially run by volunteer labour but later by female workers.
The total output of this small factory was as follows:-
4.5 in HE Shell … 63,841   60-pounder shell … 6,575
18-pounder shell … 50,784[VS]

This rear view of the Royal Children's Hospital **Heswall**, which opened in 1911, is pictured here in 1915 showing the open-plan wards which had no protection from the elements as it was then deemed healthy for the youngsters. The building was later covered in when opinions about this idea changed. The hospital closed in 1985 and a Tesco supermarket was opened on the site

George Christian's Royal Scarlet Pierrots, one of the acts that performed at **New Brighton** in 1915

Cunard Liner, " Lusitania," (Turbine).
Torpedoed and Sunk by German Submarine off
the Old Head of Kinsale, on the South Coast
of Ireland, on 7th May, 1915.
32,000 Tons; 68,000 H.P.; Speed, 26½ knots; Length 787 ft.
Breadth, 88 ft.; Depth, 60 ft.

Above: This Memorial postcard was in memory of the 1,198 lives lost when the Cunard Liner *Lusitania* sank 7 May 1915

Below: Following the sinking of the Lusitania, as many of the seamen came from Merseyside, riots broke out locally against German sounding or businesses connected to Germans. This was the damage caused to Henry Young's confectioners shop at 406 New Chester Road **Rock Ferry** and although several constables were drafted in, they were powerless against the mob that attacked the shop. In most instances the people whose premises had been attacked were innocent and had no connection with Germany

Above: Harry Lauder, the famous variety artist pictured above, appealed for recruits to join the war against Germany when appearing at the **Birkenhead** Argyle Theatre on 22 Feb[vs]

Below: This 1915 postcard is of the **New Brighton** steam-lifeboat *Queen* which operated from 1897 to 1923 and saved 196 lives. She was so named to mark the Diamond Jubilee in 1897 of Queen Victoria, patron of the RNLI. She was built with a steel hull at a cost of £4,850 by Thornycroft

—	**Storeton** Village school closed[YW8]
1 Jan	A great gale caused a building at the **Bebington** Show ground to collapse killing Pte Tinsley and injuring 11 other soldiers *(see opposite)*[VS]
1 Jan	YMCA Hut opened at **Bidston** with a New Year's Supper for 800 men[VS]
15 Jan	**Port Sunlight** Auditorium Rifle Range opened by Lieut. Col. Ellis[VS]
26 Jan	Patriotic Concert at **Little Sutton** to aid Red Cross Society[VS]
31 Jan	**Birkenhead** Tram collections for War Funds started[VS]
1 Feb	Abbotsford Red Cross Hospital opened at **Rock Ferry**[VS]
3 Feb	Neston New Auxiliary Hospital opened for inspection[VS]
19 Feb	**Rock Ferry** Red Cross Hospital opened for inspection. Hospital Flag Day[VS]
6 Mar	**Birkenhead** National Eisteddfod postponed
13 Mar	Mr AV Paton presented over 27 acres of land at **Thurstaston** as a memorial to the Wirral men who gave their lives in the Great War[VS]
16 May	**Birkenhead** Corporation employees, grave diggers, road & sanitary men return to work after two weeks strike. Wages increased[VS]
6 July	Church Street Council School **Wallasey** opened[KD]
22 Apr	Fire at Wilkies Fun Palace **New Brighton**[WON]
9 Aug	Domestic Servants' Garden Party for the wounded at **Oxton** Cricket Club[VS]
12 Aug	**Wallasey** Town Hall opened as a military hospital[VS] *(see picture opposite)*
19 Aug	**Leasowe** campers entertain war wounded[VS]
1 Oct	Warren Station **Wallasey** on the Wirral Line, closed
31 Oct	Presentation of Rowland Jackson Ambulance in **Birkenhead**[VS]

The *Rowland Jackson* ambulance was subscribed for publicly in 1916 in recognition of Mr Jackson's work as **Birkenhead's** Chief Transport Officer. Over £1,400 was raised of which £500 was set aside for the upkeep of the ambulance. This was one of several vehicles used to transport the many wounded soldiers from Woodside Station to their various hospital destinations throughout Wirral. They were also used to take the men to the entertainments provided for them at local theatres and picture houses[VS]

Above: This was the drawing of **Wallasey** Town Hall by the architects Messrs. Briggs, Wolstenholme & Thornley. The foundation stone was laid 25 March 1914 and it was opened as a military hospital 12 August 1916. By the time the hospital closed in 1919, over 3,500 wounded soldiers had been treated in the makeshift wards. The Mayor of Wallasey Alderman EG Parkinson officially opened the Town Hall 3 November 1920. The total cost of the building was £155,778

Below: This winter view of ice skating was taken at Ashton Park **West Kirby**. The park was laid out in 1899 on land rented from Miss EM Ashton who died in 1935. The council then bought her land for £3,950. As well as the lake the lower park had bowls, quoits and beautiful gardens. The upper park, across the bridge which spanned the Wirral Railway line [*now the Wirral Way*], pictured on the right, is where the famous tennis tournament was held until recently *(see 1942)*

Above: This is an exterior view of the outbuildings at *Leighton Court* in Buggen Lane **Neston** where during the First World War the owner, Mr Whineray, set up a munitions factory.

Below: An interior view of half of the main part of the munitions factory at *Leighton Court,* **Neston**

Some wounded soldiers are standing in front of The Cenacle Red Cross Hospital which stood at the top of St Georges Mount at its junction with Atherton Street **New Brighton.** Built in 1845 and known as *Sandrock*. It was bought in 1912 by a French Roman Catholic Order known as The Sisters of the Cenacle who converted it into a nunnery. The Red Cross took it over during the First World War where over 700 wounded soldiers were treated. The nuns moved to Wavertree and in the 1920s the derelict house was bought for the parishoners of SS Peter & Paul who later built a Church on the site

The funeral cortage for Private Tinsley who was killed in the **Bebington** Showground disaster 1 January 1916. The Bantams were staying in stock sheds at the showground when a fierce gale caused one of them to collapse causing many injuries[YW8]

Initially a camp was provided in the meadows below **Bidston** Hill in spring 1915 for the 3rd Battalion Cheshire Regiment and a spacious marquee was provided by the YMCA. Bidston residents clubbed together with others to provide the above comodious wooden hut for the troops on the understanding that at the close of war the hut should be handed over to Bidston Church as a Parish Hall. Strong winds had twice blown the marquee down so the opening of the YMCA Hut came non too soon on 1 January 1916 when a New Year's Supper was supplied to 800 men. The Regiment moved out at the end of 1917 and the Royal Engineers prepared the accommodation for German prisoners of war. After the war it was used as the Village Hall but was burnt down some years ago[VS]

3 Jan	**Birkenhead** Chief Constable authorised to employ paid women police[VS]
14 Feb	Opening of Auxiliary Military Hospital at **Bromborough** Golf Club house[VS]
10 Mar	Price of *Birkenhead News* increased to 1.5d (0.5p)[VS]
16 Apr	War Time Economy Food Lectures at **Birkenhead** YMCA[VS]
14 May	King George V and Queen Mary visit Cammell Laird **Birkenhead** during a two day war-time visit to Merseyside[VS]
15 May	**Wallasey** Battalion of the Cheshire Volunteers inspected by King George V[VS]
16 June	Tramway employees pay increased[VS]
12 Jul	Meeting at **Birkenhead** Town Hall re collection of waste paper[VS]
Aug	**Leasowe** Castle used house German prisoners of war for 18 months[VS]
9 Aug	Domestic servants entertain wounded – at Birknhead School **Oxton**[VS]
23 Aug	German prisoners start work on Birkett Scheme at **Bidston**[VS]
29 Aug	Sir Thomas Royden Bar, died[VS]
5 Sept	Royal National Eisteddfod held in **Birkenhead** Park. A pavilion was erected to accommodate 10,000 people. the event is marked by a Logan stone in the park[VS]
6 Sept	Prime Minister Lloyd George's visit to Wirral commences[VS]
8 Sept	Lloyd George at **Port Sunlight**[VS]
12 Sept	Wallasey Tramway Strike over employment of female drivers[TBW]
17 Oct	Grand Concert at Hemingford Military Hospital **Birkenhead**[VS]
21 Oct	Mr HN Gladstone presents badges to VAD men at **Parkgate** Hospital[VS]
22 Oct	Fire at Vernon's warehouse **Birkenhead** docks[VS]
23 Nov	Bridge Drive at St Saviour's Parish Hall **Oxton** in aid of the Bantam Battalion[VS]
27 Nov	*Mendell* at **Bromborough** opened as home for discharged sailors and soldiers[VS]
5 Dec	First woman Councillor in **Birkenhead** Miss AA Laird[VS]
29 Dec	Copies of *Birkenhead News* sent to local troops on active service[VS]

Lairds AFC of **Birkenhead**, 1st Division Liverpool Central Cup Winners 1916-17

One of the popular themes on comic postcards of this period was the newly invented Aeroplane with a suitable caption:
I am having a high time at **Birkenhead**

Below: The Auxiliary Military Hospital opened at **Bromborough** Golf Club house in early 1915. This was mainly due to the efforts of Lady Carter who was the Hon. Commandant of the Cheshire Red Cross and became Office-in-Charge here. The establishment, pictured here in 1917, was fitted up by voluntary donations with the most modern equiptment and had its own operating theatre. By February 1918 it reached its peak of 160 beds and the total number of patients treated during the four years the hospital was here amounted to 1,245. It was handed back to the golf club after the war and the course was extended to 18 holes in 1923[YW8]

Above:

Leasowe Castle housed German prisoners of war for 1·8 months from August 1917. The central tower was constructed in 1593 by the Earl of Derby and probably used for hunting purposes. It changed ownership several times being a family residence until 1895 when it became an hotel. In 1910 it was purchased for £11,750 and was opened as a Railway Convalescent Home by the Mayoress of Liverpool 12 June 1911. The castle was taken over 5 August 1914 by a local Territorial Engineers Company followed by the 3rd Battalion of the Cheshire Regiment who remained there until the prisoners of war came. It passed back to the Railway Convalescent Home in 1919 and remained in their possession until Wallasey Corporation bought it in 1970. It changed hands again in 1980 and became an hotel[RPW]

Below:

This postcard of **Parkgate**, which was published in the ERJ Wirral Series by ER Jones of Greasby, shows a group of young fishermen and one of their friends in army uniform – probably home on leave from the front, in the First World War. The tide is out so fishermen's boats can be seen beached on the sands to the left.The two buildings behind the boys were demolished in the 1960s and the site now forms the area in front of *The Old Quay* pub [*opened 1963*]. Traffic from Neston would travel along Station Road and join the Promenade at Parkgate in front of the ivy-clad building in the centre[YW6]

12 Jan	Exhibition at Allanson's store Grange Road **Birkenhead** of articles made at the British Red Cross depot, Balls Road[VS]
26 Jan	Mr Isaacson's Concert Party at Arrowe Hall Hospital **Woodchurch**[VS] (see this page)
30 Jan	Whist Drive at St Peter's Hall **Rock Ferry** for the Bantams comfort fund
14 Feb	Letter from Lord Derby regretting the necessity for breaking up or amalgamating the Wirral battalions[VS]
Mar	Masonic Lodges of **Wallasey** present Ambulance to Corporation for Red Cross purposes[VS]
9 Mar	Reception and presentation to Gourley VC at **Hoylake**[VS]
21 Mar	Meat Ration cards introduced in **Birkenhead**[VS]
8 Apr	Five day recruiting effort at **Port Sunlight** – 353 new recruits[VS]
13 Apr	Mayor & Mayoress of Birkenhead entertain wounded in **Tranmere** Military Hospital[VS]
17 Apr	*Dawpool* at **Thurstaston** opened as Military Hospital[VS] *(see picture opposite)*
23 Apr	Zeebrugge Raid - **Wallasey** ferry boats *Daffodil & Iris* involved and due the bravery of their crews, were susequently given the title Royal[VS]
10 May	Woodlands School **Birkenhead** sale of work for Red Cross[VS]
17 May	**Wallasey** ferry boats Iris & Daffodil arrive in Mersey after their Zeebrugge feat[VS] *(see opposite)*
4 June	Lieut. W Ashcroft bequeaths £500 for War Memorial, Birkenhead School **Oxton**[VS]
7 June	Sale of soldier's needlework at **Tranmere** Military Hospital[VS]
1 July	Coal Rationing Order comes into force[VS]
13 July	French Red Cross Day. Case of Clicquot Champagne (1906) auctioned by the Mayor of **Birkenhead** for £155 in aid of funds[VS]
7 Sept	Duchess of Westminster opens Garden fete at **Bromborough** Military Hospital[VS]
14 Sept	Baseball match at **Bebington** – Americans v Canadians[VS]
25 Sept	Explosion in the West Float **Wallasey** five men killed and several injured[VS]
12 Oct	Frank Lester from **Irby** was killed in action and was later awarded a Posthumous V.C. for his action *(see this page)*[YW6]
17 Oct	**Birkenhead's** War Saving record now over one million pounds[VS]
11 Nov	*Armistice Day* - 'The war to end all wars' had come to its victorious finish and 'never again' was the hope. Jubilant scenes in Hamilton Square **Birkenhead**[VS]
18 Nov	Wilfred Owen the **Birkenhead** poet was killed
21 Dec	Dr McDonald elected first member of Parliament for **Wallasey**[KD]

Frank Lester, aged 22, son of John and Ellen Lester market gardners of *Miller's Hey* **Irby**, who was with the 10th Battalion Lancashire Fusilliers was awarded a postumous VC for his bravery at the village of Neuvilly on 12 October 1918 when he sacraficed his life to save the life of others [there is a plaque in Irby Library to commemorate his deed]. Prior to the war he had been the organist at the Primative Methodist Church in Irby[YW6]

This postcard was sent from Arrowe Hall, **Woodchurch**, during the First World War when it was used as a Military Hospital. Mr Isaacson held a concert party here 26 January 1918[VS]

The TSS *Iris* and her sister ship the Daffodil were built for **Wallasey** Corporation in 1906. Both ships became famous for their exploits at Zeebrugge 23 April 1918 (the *Iris* is seen here in her war-time cladding) and upon return they were both granted *Royal* prefixes for their endeavours. The bullet-ridden funnel of the Iris stood at **Seacombe** Ferry for many years

Above: *Dawpool* which was built in 1884 for Thomas Ismay, the founder of the White Star Line, is pictured in **Thurstaston** prior to World War One. The property and its land passed out of the family after Thomas Ismay's wife Margaret died 9 April 1907. Members of the family were offered the chance of living there but there were no takers as the building was too big, very cold and draughty.

On 17 April 1918 the property was loaned by the then owner, Mr FWP Rutter who was manager of the London & Lancs Fire Insurance, to be used as an orthopedic hospital for officers. The last function was a Garden Party for the Hoylake & West Kirby Cottage Hospital 18 September 1926 which raised £300. There was no interest in buying the house at auction so the interior and exterior fittings were sold and the remaining building was dynamited 16 May 1927. The site of Dawpool was the opposite side of Thurstaston Road from the *Cottage Loaf*

This photograph of the 2nd Birkenhead Scout Troop was taken in 1918 outside their headquarters

—	Theatre Royal Argyle Street **Birkenhead** sold to a cinema company
—	**Leasowe** became a popular place to live as it was unrated
—	**Prenton** War Memorial dedicated
—	Sir David Beatty visits **Wallasey** and unveils the bronze tablets on the Royals Iris & Daffodil[KD]
Mar	**Rock Ferry** Auxiliary Military Hospital closed[VS]
2 June	Demolition of the steel structure part of **New Brighton** Tower commenced
12 July	First motor bus route commenced between **Rock Ferry** Pier and Park Station **Birkenhead**[TBW]
19 July	Peace Celebrations[KD]
1 Aug	**Birkenhead** Police joined the national strike over pay and conditions. This was followed by looting and rioting then on the 2/3 August 500 troops arrived in the town. On 18 August peace was restored and the troops withdrawn. All sergeants and constables who had taken part in the strike were dismissed. New pay scales were introduced by the end of August. **Wallasey** Police had refused to join in the police strike[MQP]
2 Aug	Bread Strike begins in **Wallasey**
4 Oct	Dedication of the **New Brighton** War memorial[KD]

Below: This postcard view taken by The Aircraft Manufacturing Co Ltd of Hendon in 1919 shows **New Brighton** pier in the foreground jutting out into the River Mersey and to the right is New Brighton Tower with the top partly dismantled. Due to the lack of maintainance during the 1914-18 war, the 1,000 ton steel structure was considered to be unsafe and was dismantled between May 1919 and June 1921

Above: This was the resting place for the white Ensign pictured here in St Mary's Church **Birkenhead** on 15 January 1919. It was used in the Great War by HMS *Birkenhead*

Above: Bidston Windmill, which is pictured on Bidston Hill in 1919, dates back to the late 18th century and was last worked in 1875. It is still there today. The bridge on the left in Vyner Road joins the two halves of Bidston Hill. This 46 acre estate was opened to the public as a recreational area in 1894

Below: A 1919 advert for Robb Bros of Grange Road **Birkenhead** showing the fashion of the day[vs]

— Application made by the three policewomen in the **Birkenhead** Police Force to be placed on the same scale as men. The Chief Constable stated that in his experience "they were only fit for the lighter parts of police work and that they are considerably below the value of policemen". Two of the policewomen then resigned and the remaining one left the force in March 1921[MQP]

— **Bidston** war Memorial unveiled

— Bed endowed at **Wallasey** Central Hospital to commemorate Zeebrugge Battle[KD]

— New Film Studio opened at **Seacombe**[KD]

— Revival of **Wallasey** Carnival[KD]

— Spragg's Vale Brewery, Leasowe Road, **Wallasey Village** bought out by Higsons

— The Chrysanthemums of **Wallasey** performed their first pantomine *Slave of the Lamp* in aid of local charities

— Following the strike by **Birkenhead** police in August 1919, the Chief Constable reported that "the force had improved in both contentment, efficiency and discipline"

14 Feb   Sir Thomas Royden unveiled the War memorial at St Johns Church **Frankby** *(see this page)*

25 Mar   **Thingwall** Hall gifted in Miss MC Twigge's will as a country home for sick children *(see this page)*

31 Mar   **Bidston** Aerodrome opened (see this page)

3 April   First **Wallasey** Bus service - from **Seacombe** Ferry to Harrison Drive[TBW]

11 Sept   Oldershaw Schools for Girls & Boys were opened as additional **Wallasey** secondary schools[WON]

20 Oct   Outbreak of fire at Tivoli Theatre, **New Brighton** with £1,000 damage[KD]

3 Nov   **Wallasey** Town Hall opened[RPW]

2 Dec   Mammoth crane lifted 150 ton gangway at **New Brighton** *(see opposite page)*

Thingwall Hall was built in 1849 for a Captain Lilley in 21 acres of land at the junction of Thingwall Road and Barnston Road. This imposing house changed hands several times and at the turn of the previous century it was bought by a Mr Twigge and it was his daughter, Muriel, who gave the hall to the Royal Liverpool Children's Hospital 25 March 1920 and who became matron during the 1920s. The hall was demolished in the 1960s and the Thingwall Corner Council Estate was built on the site

Bidston Aerodrome opened 31 March 1920 organised by Great Northern Syndicate Ltd. The Golden Eagle Aviation Co Ltd used GE1 (a war machine of the De Haviland type - modified and adapted for passengers and DH6 a WW1 aeroplane)

Above: Sir Thomas Royden is seen speaking about Frankby & District war heros on the occasion of the unveiling of the War Memorial at **Frankby** Church. There were 27 members of the parish killed in the First World War and the names of the 19 who fell in the Second World War were added in 1950. The Vicar, Rev Sanderson, is seen under the lychgate

Above: Looking up Pensby Road **Heswall** *c.*1920, the single storied shop on the right was the Bon Bon and opposite was Tarbuck's Fish, Game & Poultry shop whose letterhead is seen on the left

Left: A 1920 letterhead for Tarbuck's *(see above)*

A crowd has gathered to watch the giant crane *Mammoth* lift the 150 ton gangway for **New Brighton** Pier on 2 Dec 1920. The gangway was to connect the floating stage with the pier which is seen on the right

This view of the camping ground at **Leasowe,** taken from the top of Leasowe lighthouse, was on a postcard sent in 1920. The population of Leasowe had increased from 989 in 1911 to 4,029 by 1921 due to the shortage of housing locally after the First World War and this area being rate-free. *Bankfield House* is seen in the foreground surrounded not only by tents but other properties which had then started to become permanent. A similar view a year later would reveal that the ground where the tents are sited would be totally engulfed with huts, converted railway carriages, caravans etc. However, this land was low lying and prone to flooding so most of the dwellings had to be raised off the ground to avoid this

—	Holy Name R.C. Church, Beresford Road **Oxton** consecrated[DoS]
—	Lever Bros Holiday Camp opened at **Thurstaston**
—	Work completed by **Wallasey** Council on building 33 houses in Alderley Road
—	Municipal Maternity Home opened in Mill Lane Hospital **Wallasey**[MM]
1 Jan	**Seacombe** Ferry Fare increased to 3d [1p][KD]
26 Jan	War Memorial on Magazine Promenade **Egremont** to theWallasey men who died in WW1 unveilled *(see page 64)* [KD]
Mar	Bus service commenced between Charing Cross, **Birkenhead**, and **Seacombe** Ferry[TBW]
30 April	**Moreton** Picture House opened (see this page)
22 June	Launching of Liscard, first luggage ferry steamer for **Wallasey** Corporation to transport vehicles across the Mersey *(see this page)*[WCS]
22 June	**New Brighton** steel tower finally demolished[KD]
15 Aug	Alwen Water Scheme comleted and opened supplying water to **Birkenhead** from N. Wales
19 Aug	*King Orry*, Isle of Man steamer, ran aground at **New Brighton** *(see opposite)*[KD]
10 Sept	Mr Pat Collins Jun purchases Tivoli Theatre, **New Brighton**[KD]
10 Sept	Disaster at Clover Clayton's Dry Dock, **Birkenhead** when five apprentices were killed whilst dismantling the ex-German Submarine *Deutschland*
Oct	Bus service commenced between Charing Cross **Birkenhead** and **Liscard** Village[WB]
11 Nov	James Williams a **Birkenhead** fireman was injured when a maroon blew up at Hamilton Square for the Armistace Day Gun Salute in front of the Town Hall
16 Nov	James Williams a **Birkenhead** fireman died following an injury on Armistice Day in front of the Town Hall *(see photo page 60)*
31 Dec	New Telephone Exchange opened **Liscard**[KD]

The Luggage Ferry DTSS *Liscard*, which was built by Thornycroft & Co of Southampton for **Wallasey** Corporation, was launched 22 June 1920. Several vehicles, including a Scotts of Bootle van, can be seen aboard this first luggage ferry built for Wallasey Corporation. The DTSS *Liscard* and her sister ship DTSS Leasowe were both built in 1921 to provide improved facilities for the transport of an increasing number of vehicles wanting to cross the Mersey. The vessels had a very large funnel together with deck house and high bridge in the centre of the boat which gave maximum parking space for vehicles. The vehicular ferry service lost a lot of its custom when the Mersey Road Tunnel was opened in 1934 but continued until it finally closed in March 1947. However, in 1941 The Liscard was requisitioned and fitted with a large crane to assist in quick unloading of aircraft from merchant ships and was sold in 1946 to D/S A/S Hetland, Copenhagen and renamed *Lisca*

Below: Crowds are proceeding down Station Road **Moreton** (later renamed Pasture Road) towards Leasowe Shore. They are passing Ye Olde English Picture House which was officially opened 30 April 1921

Population Census 1921

Arrowe	106	Moreton-cum-Lingham	4,029
Barnston	793	Ness	527
Bebington Hr	1,765	Neston-cum-Parkgate UD	5,195
Bebington Lr	14,687	Noctorum	192
Bidston	899	Pensby	92
Birkenhead	145,577	Poulton-cum-Spital	548
Brimstage	183	Prenton	1,328
Bromborough	2,652	Puddington	299
Burton	282	Raby	394
Caldy	266	Saughall Massie	315
Capenhurst	139	Shotwick	76
Childer Thornton	851	Storeton	279
Eastham	10,098	Sutton, Great	421
Frankby	255	Sutton, Little	1,635
Gayton	219	Thingwall	416
Grange	665	Thornton Hough	598
Greasby	585	Thurstaston	207
Heswall-cum-Oldfield	4,349	Upton	1,132
Hooton	204	Wallasey	90,809
Hoylake & West Kirby UD	17,068	Whitby	13,063
Irby	233	Willaston	997
Landican	75	Woodchurch	129
Ledsham	152		

The Manx Steamer *King Orry* was launched at Cammell Laird **Birkenhead** 11 March 1913. She saw duty during the First World War including being present at the surrender of the German High Seas Fleet on 21 November 1918 and later returned to her Isle of Man duties. Arriving in thick Mersey Fog from Douglas on 19 August 1921 she ran aground close to Perch Rock and **New Brighton** Lighthouse (seen on the left). The Wallasey Fire Brigade are rendering useful service to the full complement of stranded passengers by placing their ladders against the ship so passengers could leave if they wanted to. However, later that evening she was towed to safety at high tide and was back in service within four days. She was lost at Dunkirk 29 May 1940[YW4]

The **Birkenhead** fire engine is pictured outside 3 Tansley Terrace Newton Cross Lane **Newton**, the home of James Williams, a Birkenhead fireman. He died 16 November 1921 following an injury when a maroon blew up at Hamilton Square for the Armistice Day Gun Salute in front of the Town Hall on 11 November

The **Port Sunlight** War Memorial, where The Causeway and The Diamond intersect, was designed & sculptured by Sir W Goscombe John 1916-21

Wallasey War Memorial is pictured on Magazine promenade **New Brighton.** Sculptured by Birnie Rhind of Edinburgh, the memorial was unveiled by Lord Dery 26 January 1921 in memory of 848 men of the borough who died in World War One[RPW]

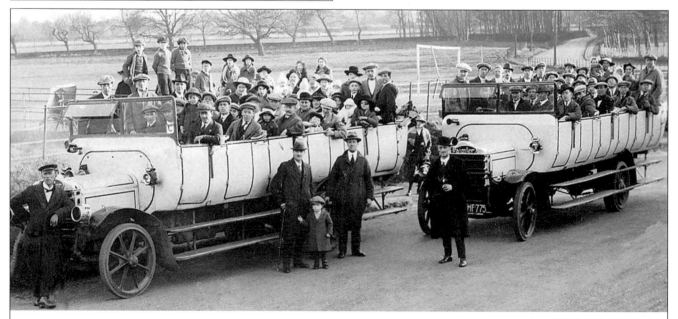

Rock Ferry Comrades FC and supporters are posing for a photograph in front of The Green at **Thornton Hough** 24 April 1924

— 1922 was a year of widespread unemployment with Government departments making economies. **Birkenhead** Police had to comply and reduced the strength of the force; reducing uniform issues; reducing rent, boot and plain clothes allowences and a 2.5% reduction in the pay of all ranks[MQP]

— Star Yachts (Model Boats) founded by Franz Denye in **Birkenhead**[BPH]

— All blind people to travel free on **Wallasey** Ferries

— St Agnes RC Church consecrated at **West Kirby**[DoS]

31 Jan   **New Ferry** ferry service closed

5 Feb   **Oxton** Congregational Church gutted by fire

15 Apr   **Upton** Racecourse opened on Moreton Road between Upton & Moreton [now the Upton Spur Road for the M53 Motorway][YW7]

1 June   Trocadero Cinema **New Brighton** opened[KD]

28 July   World Cycling Championship run at **New Brighton** Tower Grounds[WON]

Dec   Lower Lighthouse **Hoylake** demolished (see 1894) [KD]

16 Dec   War Memorial dedicated **West Kirby** *(see page 66)*

16 Dec   Lady Lever Art Gallery **Port Sunlight** opened by Princess Beatrice

This is the South entrance to Lady Lever Art Gallery which was opened 16 December 1922 by Princess Beatrice

Oxton Road Congregational Church is pictured in Woodchurch Road **Birkenhead** (to the left) taken from Oxton Road with Balls Road to the right of the Church. Originally built 1857-8 by William Cole, it was gutted by fire 5 February 1922 and rebuilt, re-opening 27 September 1923. The four pinacles have since been removed[BPH]

ET Browning's old horse-drawn delivery carts are pictured outside their baker's shop at 186 Wallasey Road **Wallasey** together with their modern delivery vans. Founded just before the First World War, the business continued here until the late 1930s. They also had other branches at 77 King Street, 128a Rake Lane and 8 Rowson Street

West Kirby War Memorial erected on Grange Hill is an obelisk flanked by two bronze figures which was designed by CS Jagger and dedicated to the local men who lost their lives in the First World War. There is also a memorial to those who perished in the Second World War

Comic postcard of the time sent from **West Kirby**

— Sacred Heart Catholic Church opened in **Moreton**[DoS]

— Wirral Railway absorbed into the London, Midland and Scottish Group of Railways[KD]

— New Nave at St Columba's Church **Egremont** opened and Consecrated by the Bishop of Chester[KD]

12 Jan Dixie Dean played his first game for **Tranmere** Rovers having been transferred from **Pensby** FC for a reputed fee of a set of jerseys! *(see this page)*[YW1]

30 April Captain AC Dawson appointed the new Chief Constable of **Birkenhead**[MQP]

27 Sept Oxton Road Congregational Church **Birkenhead** re-opened following restoration after fire

Oct **Birkenhead** Police purchased a four-speed motor cycle combination for £91. This was the founding of the 'modern' Traffic Department[MQP]

1 Oct LMS inaugurate 'Through Train Service' from **New Brighton** to Euston[KD]

Below:

The Edward VII Memorial Clock is pictured from Argyle Street **Birkenhead** *c.*1923. The clock, which was designed by Edmund Kirby & Sons, was unveiled in 1912. The monument was moved *c.*1929 to its present site in Clifton Crescent to make way for the approach roads for the Mersey Tunnel

Dixie Dean, pictured here in his England shirt, originally played for **Pensby** FC from the age of 14. He stayed there for two years before being transferred to **Tranmere** Rovers. His first game for them was 12 January 1923 and his last 14 March 1924 when he was transferred to Everton FC aged 17. In his 27 league appearances for Tranmere Rovers in the 1923/24 season he scored 27 goals[TR2]

—	Open Golf Championship held at Royal Liverpool Golf Club, **Hoylake**[RLGC]
—	Fire at Paul Bros Grain Warehouse, **Wallasey**[KD]
—	Opening of Wallasey Grange, Grove Road, **Wallasey** as a municipal golf house[KD]
—	Opening of Gorsey Lane, **Wallasey**, the new Highway Link between **Wallasey** & **Birkenhead** at a cost of £14,800[KD]
—	The Cosmo picture House, **Wallasey Village**, re-opened as a Theatre re-named The Coliseum[KD]
—	New Central Liberal Club opened in Church Street **Egremont** by Viscount Leverhulme. Cost £4,000[KD]
—	Milk War in **Wallasey** - Dispute between Farmers and Milk Dealers lasted two weeks and milk retailed at 2d per quart below usual price[KD]
—	**Upton** racecourse, Moreton Road, Upton purchased by Wallasey Corporation - 111.5 acres for £30,335 17s 6d[KD]
20 Jan	**Heswall** Golf Clubhouse, which was constructed entirely from pitch pine was burnt down. The estimated damage was put at £10,000[YW6]
14 Mar	Dixie Dean played his last game for **Tranmere** Rovers *(see picture opposite)*[TRFC]
23 April	Empire Exhibition at Wembley opened
June	An attempt on Mount Everest resulted in the death of Mr Leigh-Mallory and Mr AC Irvine (both of **Birkenhead**). A report of 21st June said they were last seen within 800 ft of the summit - it may never be known whether they were the first to conquor Everest *(see below)*

OPEN-AIR
GYM. DISPLAYS
BY
Y.M.C.A. Gym. Members
IN BIRKENHEAD PARK
(Balaclava Ground)
On THURSDAY, 28th AUGUST, 1924,
At 7-30 p.m., ALSO IN
VICTORIA PARK (TRANMERE)
ON
MONDAY, 1st SEPTEMBER, 1924,
At 7-30 p.m.

The **POST OFFICE MILITARY BAND** *will play at Birkenhead Park.*

Y.M.C.A. GYM. PARTICULARS.
Gym. re-opens 20th September, 1924, at 7-45 p.m.
CLASSES and FEES :

	Y.M.	Gym.	Total
Seniors (under 21) -	7/6	7/6	15/-
„ (over 21) -	10/-	10/-	20/-
Juniors (Boys under 17)	5/-	2/6	7/6
Ladies - - - -		7/6	per quarter
Junior Ladies - -		6/-	,,
Girls - - - -		5/-	,,
Boys - - - -		5/-	,,

H. COURTENAY BICKLEY, *Hon. Sec.*
CHAS. LORD, B.A.P.T., M.I.H.
W. H. RALSTON, *Gen. Sec.*

The 1924 British Everest Expedition ended in tragedy when Andrew Comyn Irvine and George Leigh-Mallory, both with local connections, died near the summit of Everest. Andrew 'Sandy' Irvine was born in Birkenhead in 1902 and was educated at Birkenhead Preparatory School & Birkenhead Junior School from 1910–16 before completing his education at Shrewsbury School; his father was William Fergusson Irvine, also an old boy of Birkenhead School, a well known authority on local history with many publications to his name. George Leigh-Mallory's father was the Vicar of the Church of St John, Huskinson Street, off Grange Road **Birkenhead** *(see also 1896)*. It was at 12.50pm on Sunday 8 June 1924 that Noel Odell, another member of the team, saw the distant figures of Irvine and Mallory on the North East Ridge within striking distance of the summit. His view of them vanished when they became enveloped in cloud once more. What happened to them then entered into mountaineering legend. Did either or both of them make the summit 29 years before Edmond Hillary and Tenzing Norgay?

Three roads off Borough Road in **Prenton** were named to commemorate the event – Mallory Road, Irvine Road and Everest Road.

On the 75th anniversary in 1999, an Anglo–American team traced the footsteps of the 1924 British Everest Expedition. They found Mallory's preserved body 2,000 feet from the summit but no evidence to confirm if they made the summit. Perhaps one day Irvine's body with their camera will be found and the question answered

Andrew Irvine (left), pictured with George Leigh–Mallory (right) who were members of the 1924 British Everest Expedition

The photographer had his back to St Mary's Parish Church at **Eastham** and was looking towards the *Hooton Arms* in **Eastham** Village, the ivy-covered building in the distance, which by 1860 had become a beerhouse with Catherine Hazlehurst the victualler. The construction of the Manchester Ship Canal from 1887 to 1894 brought problems to the area with an influx of construction workers but this must have brought great financial rewards to the owners of the local hostelries. The newsagent and general stores, with the bill boards outside, is on the left and the Post Office is behind the delivery vehicle[YW9]

The original miller's cottage *(see 1898)* is pictured at the junction of what is now Mill Lane **Irby** (right) and Hillbark Road (left). It was purchased by the George & Bertha Lumsden in 1919 and is pictured here in 1924, the year they opened it as The Old Mill Cafe and Stores. Known locally for many decades as Lumsden's Cafe, they held dances here two to three times a week. The land and buildings were purchased in 1938 by Higson's Brewery but the site was not developed due to planning permission being refused. However, eventually planning permission was granted in the 1970s but on condition that the cottage should be saved and any extensions in keeping with the existing property. *The Mill* pub opened in 1980

- **New Brighton** open air theatre now enclosed and named the Floral Pavilion[RPW]
- **Rock Ferry** & Park High (**Birkenhead**) schools for boys established
- **Wallasey** South Branch Library, in Borough Road, opened[RPW]
- Work completed on building 171 houses for **Wallasey** Council houses in Mill Lane. Rental in 1934 was 16/6d [82p] per week inclusive
- *SS Upton* built by Cammell Laird **Birkenhead** for **Rock Ferry** to Liverpool route. When the service closed 1939 it transfered to Woodside as a back-up boat[WCS]
- *Oxton & Bidston* – luggage boats launched at Cammell Laird **Birkenhead** for the transportation of vehicular traffic across the Mersey. Following the opening of the Mersey Tunnel trade declined on this route and the service closed July 1941. The boats were then fitted with a crane and used in the war effort to unload aircraft in mid river from ships from America

5 Feb	New wing of the Liverpool Open-air Hospital for Children opened at **Leasowe**
2-4 May	Old landing stage at **Seacombe** replaced[TBW]
18 May	Referendum for **Birkenhead** Ratepayers on Mersey Tunnel Bill - in favour by majority of over 4:1
5 July	Cenotaph in Hamilton Square **Birkenhead** unveilled in memory of the 1,293 men of **Birkenhead** who fell in service during World War One *(see next page)*
16 Dec	The first Mersey Tunnel shaft sunk at the Ceremonial Inauguration by HRH Princess Mary Viscount Lascelles
17 Dec	Princess Mary launched the battleship *HMS Rodney* at Cammell Laird **Birkenhead**[MOI]

ARGYLE
THEATRE, BIRKENHEAD.
Sole Proprietor . . . . . D. J. CLARKE.

6-40 MONDAY, MARCH 2nd, 1925, **8-50**
And Twice Nightly during the Week.

From the Alhambra, London.

RUDINOFF
The Celebrated Artiste, in a Novel Studio Entertainment.
ARTIST.   SMOKE PAINTER.   SIFFLEUR.

CYCLING BRUNETTES
In their Laughable Novelty, "DEFYING GRAVITY."

VANWY CHARD
The Favorite Welsh Songstress.

RENE & RENARD
In their Musical Act, featuring the Banjo.

IKE FREEDMAN
Character Entertainer, in Italian and Hebrew Studies.

The 2 CARRS | **Peggy HOLMES**
Vocalists and Dancers. | Comedienne and Dancer.

Fred HASTINGS
The Cowboy Ventriloquist, and his Loquacious Friend, "FREDDY."

BROWN'S ROYAL BIOSCOPE.

TERRY WILSON
The Favorite Light Comedian, in a New Act.

MUSICAL INTERLUDE BY THE ARGYLE ORCHESTRA

Popular Prices,   Box Office open fro   a.m. to 10 p.m.
Telephones—1524 & 1525 Birkenhead.

A typical Argyle Theatre **Birkenhead** programme with nine variety acts, the Argyle Orchestra during the interlude and Brown's Royal Bioscope (a short cinematic show)

These houses in Osmaston Road **Prenton** are pictured having just been completed in 1925. The Prenton War Memorial on the right was erected in 1919 as a memorial to the men of Prenton who gave their lives in the First World War. It was reconstructed following bomb damage in 1940 and the names of those men who gave their lives in the Second World War were added

The crowds have gathered to witness the unveiling service of the Cenotaph in Hamilton Square **Birkenhead** on 5 July 1925 in memory of the 1,293 men of Birkenhead who gave their lives in the First World War. It replaced the John Laird Statue which had been erected here in 1877 and was moved to its present site at the other end of the square. This caused controversy at the time as the statue of Birkenhead's first MP and whose family had helped the town to develop, now had his back on the town hall

The Mammoth lifting a boom at **Seacombe** Ferry 2 May 1925[TRW]

— Additional water to supply **Wallasey** from Lake Alwen North Wales agreed with Birkenhead Corporation[RPW]

— **Birkenhead** Borough Hospital in Park Road North changed its name to Birkenhead General Hospital[YW2]

— Work completed for **Wallasey** Council, building a total of 115 houses in Surrey Street & Mostyn Street

— Mission Church opened in Pasture Road **Moreton** to serve Caravan Dwellers *(See this page)*

— **Birkenhead** Amateur Operatic Society first performance In the Days of Good Queen Bess

4 Jan   The foundation stone was laid for St Catherine & Martina Roman Catholic Church, Birkenhead Road **Hoylake**

3-12 May General Strike - Police escort for **Birkenhead** Corporation buses (see this page)[BB]
Birkenhead was more fortunate than other parts of the country during the General Strike where only two persons were before the court for disorder arising out of that crisis[MQP]

June   New **Heswall** Golf Clubhouse opened. This replaced the wooden clubhouse burnt down *(see 1924)*[YW6]

Aug   Lord Leverhulme sold 425 acres of **Arrowe Park** to Birkenhead Corporation

21 Aug   Poulton Bridge became Toll Free

4 Sept   Capitol Cinema opened at **Liscard**[SS2]

23 Oct   New Landing Stage & three-track Floating Roadway installed at **Seacombe** which cost £204,000 was opened by Lord Derby[RPW]

The Mission Church opened in Pasture Road on land given by Lady Vyner at the corner of Ditton Lane **Moreton** to serve caravan dwellers. The area being low-lying was prone to flooding as seen here when the building was surrounded by water. The Mission Church was dismantled in 1938

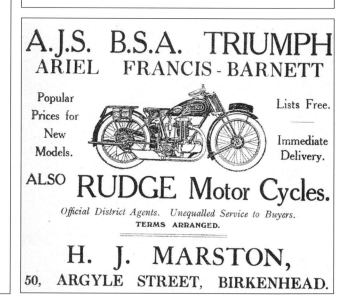

The Birkenhead Corporation No 19 bus is pictured at **Prenton** tram terminus facing down Prenton Road West with Prenton Congregational Church in the background. This Leyland G7 single decker bus was one of six which saw service from 1923 to 1928-9. However, this photograph was taken during the General Strike in May 1926 when the bus had wire mesh protection over the windows and police escort vehicle (pictured behind). The group standing in front of the bus includes Luke Lees, second from right, who was the volunteer driver[BB]

This brand new Sentinel Steam Wagon DG4, which was built for James Crutchley, Coal Merchant and Haulage Contractor, based at 2 Argyle South **Birkenhead**, is seen ready to leave the Senitel Works *c.*1926

This Sentinel Steam Wagon DG4 Tipper, which was built for Wm Roebuck Haulage Removals of Radnor Avenue & Pensby Road **Heswall**, is similar to the James Crutchley vehicle seen above but this is the tipper version and is also ready to leave the Senitel Works *c.*1926

— *ss Wallasey and Marlowe* came into service for **Wallasey** Corporation[WCS]

— Celebrations to mark **Birkenhead** Borough's 50th anniversary 1877–1927 *(see opposite page)*[B]

— Birkenhead School **Oxton** held an Elizabethan Fayre to celebrate the Borough's 50th anniversary *(see opposite page)*[OIH]

12 Mar **Ness** Colliery finally closed

9 May **Port Sunlight** Station opened for public use[RSW]

23 May 6th Birkenhead Company Boys Brigade formed at **Tranmere**

Oct School for Delicate Children transferred from Lawrence Road to the Elleray Park premises in **New Brighton** with accommodation for[RPW]

Above:

This photograph was taken at Woodside terminus **Birkenhead** in 1927 and shows a conductor standing by a No 9 New Ferry tram. This was one of the original 13 New Ferry tramcars which were single-deck due to the low bridge that spanned Chester Street near Cammell Laird. Following the popularity of the service they were all converted to double-deckers by 1910 but with a low headroom and flat roof because of the problem bridge. These trams were modified several times but a year after the service was abandoned in 1931, the bodies were broken up but the frames and bogies were said to have been exported to India

Left:

This advertisement for JH Mycock's Harvest Bread could be as relevant today as then because the present owners, Hurst's Bakery of **Birkenhead**, produce excellent bread made by a local firm with local labour

Some locals are examining the damage caused to the boat which was beached at **Meols** following a storm on 28 October 1927

This former **Birkenhead** Corporation horse tram was one of two trams chosen to represent both eras of Birkenhead's public tram system as part of the procession to illustrate the development of passenger transport during the previous 50 years for the Birkenhead Borough Jubilee celebrations of 1927. The horse-drawn era was from 1860, when Birkenhead operated the first public tram system in Europe, to 1901 when the system changed to electric trams. The driver and passengers are dressed in costumes that would have been worn in 1860 when Birkenhead became the first town in Europe to operate a public tram system

As with the photograph above, these boys from Birkenhead School **Oxton** are celebrating **Birkenhead** Borough's Jubilee in 1927. They are taking part in an Elizabethan Fayre where Queen Elizabeth I is knighting one of her subjects[OIH]

— Alfred McAlpine & Sons Ltd established in Cambridge Road **Ellesmere Port**[EP]

— **Birkenhead** Borough boundaries extended to include **Landican, Thingwall, Prenton** and part of **Bidston**

— Egerton Grove school **Wallasey** built[WON]

— **Neston** Colliery closed

— North-End sub Fire Station opened in Laird Street **Birkenhead** near St James Church[KD]

— **Oxton** Cricket Club purchased their ground in Townfield Lane for £4,000 *(see this page)*

— *Red Lion Inn* **Willaston** ceased being a public house *(see opposite)*[YW8]

— SS Catherine & Martina RC Church opened Birkenhead Road **Meols**[DoS]

— Wallasey Corporation bought **New Brighton** pier after it was condemned by the Board of Trade[WON]

— **Wallasey** Council completed 94 houses in the Hillcroft Estate & 270 in Gorsedale Road (20 being flats)[WON]

25 Mar St Thomas' Church foundation stone laid **Wallasey**[WON]

1 Apr **Wallasey** Corporation now incorporated **Leasowe, Moreton** & part of **Bidston**[WON]

1 Apr Bus route established between Bermuda Road **Moreton** from **Seacombe** and **New Brighton** Ferries[WB]

3 April Tunnels from **Birkenhead** and Liverpool met and broke through under the River Mersey

Dec Well Lane, **Tranmere**, Police Station opened with a number of Police houses attached[MQP]

1 Dec Williamson Art Gallery opened in Slatey Road **Birkenhead**[B]

Negotiations for Oxton Cricket Club to buy their ground in Townfield Lane, **Oxton** began in 1920 but it was not until 1928 that they purchased the land from the Earl of Shrewsbury for £4,000. The pavilion on the left was completed in 1883. St Saviour's Church is pictured in the background

Right top: The Roman Catholic Church of St Catherine & Martina was opened in Birkenhead Road **Hoylake** in 1928. It was built by Smith Bros. of Hoylake for the Hoylake & Meols worshipers who had previously travelled to St Agnes Church in West Kirby[DoS]

Below: This picture postcard view of **Irby** Village was sent in 1928. The only changes from the previous century were the building in the distance, the *Prince of Wales* inn, which ceased being a pub after the First World War and the newly completed building with the canopy was the Irby Stores. This shop, which was owned by Arthur Constantine, was the first of several shops to be built which catered for the increasing population of this once quiet village. The three cottages on the left were lived in at this time by the Singleton's, Shaws and Andrews with the single-storied, thatched Post Office beyond being owned by a Mr ER Jones, whose daughter ran it for him

Above: The *Red Lion Hotel*, which faced the village green in **Willaston**, became a public house in the early 1800s although a date stone places the building back to at least 1631. It ceased being a public house in 1928 and plans to demolish the building and replace it with a new one were turned down in 1972. It then went to auction and was bought and restored as a private dwelling

Below: The Williamson Art Gallery in Slatey Road **Birkenhead**, which opened 1 December 1928, was the result of the bequest of John Williamson, a former Commissioner for Birkenhead who left £20,000 in his will for the erection of a museum and art gallery to be paid on the death of his son. However, his son survived him by only four years and directed that a further £20,000 be added towards the project

— **Birkenhead** Library built in 1909 and was demolished in 1929 to make way for the Mersey Tunnel approach roads

— Cole Street school opened in **Birkenhead**

— The Belvidere Road **Wallasey** housing scheme completed. Prices for the 128 houses ranged from £730 to £760

— **Egremont** Ferry reconstructed

— New Bandstand built in **Birkenhead** Park

— Holding the World Scout Jamboree at Arrowe Park caused the **Birkenhead** Police a great deal of extra and arduous work. To alleviate some of the pressure a strong detachment of Police from Liverpool arrived to help out[MQP]

31 July   World Jamboree of Boy Scouts opened at **Arrowe Park** - some 50,000 boy scouts gathered from 31 July to 13 August[DA]

1 Aug   Prince of Wales arrived at the Jamboree via **Hooton** Aerodrome[DA]

Oct   Bus service between **New Brighton** & **New Ferry** commenced[WB]

Right: The original Hillbark at **Frankby** was a mansion of red sandstone in Gothic style which was erected in 1868-70 and enlarged 1882. By 1923 it was the residence of Mrs Smith, Ernest Royden's mother-in law from whom he purchased the property set in 150 acres of land in 1925

Below: The 'new' Hillbark at **Frankby** is seen on the site of the original one which Ernest Royden had demolished. It started life as Bidston Court in Vyner Road Bidston which was owned by Royden. He transported it brick by brick over three years from 1929-31, then re-naming it after the previous building

Above: The Boy Scouts of America gateway is pictured at the **Arrowe** Park International Scout Jamboree which took place from 31 July to 13 August 1929. This venue was chosen as 1929 was the 21st anniversary of the inaugural meeting of the Boy Scout Movement at Birkenhead YMCA, Grange Road on 24 January 1908. This photograph must have been taken in the early part of the fortnight as most of the 320,000 paying public who visited the camp suffered from the effects of continuous rain which made the ground underfoot very wet and the event was unofficially re-named 'mudboree'[DA]

Left: This cartoon by Sid Wright was one the 'Tommy the Tenderfoot' series of comic postcards produced by Winstanley & Watkins of Liverpool especially for the **Arrowe** Park Jamboree

Below: The poor children of Charles Thompson Mission **Birkenhead** are eating their lunch at Lever Bros holiday camp at Thurstaston. This was an annual event when the Lever Bros employees treated the children. This site at Thurstaston, which was the river side of the railway line and overlooked the River Dee and Welsh coast, was purchased by Lever Bros in 1919 and opened in 1921. The Lever Bros Employees' Handbook of 1930 states:

> ***HOLIDAY CAMP – THURSTASTON.*** *A Camp by the sea has been established. Excellent huts, comfortably equipped, are provided and will at present accommodate 200 people. Tennis, football, cricket, basket ball and other games are provided for, and there is good sea bathing.*
> *Full particulars can be obtained from the notice boards or the Service Department*

HIS STAFF OF LIFE.

SID WRIGHT

1929
14

— The Road Traffic Act, 1930, gave a grant to all Police Forces to purchase and maintain motor vehicles for traffic purposes. **Birkenhead** bought three new motor cycle combinations for traffic patrol, transferring six policemen[MQP]

— **New Brighton** pier reopens after repairs and re-modernisation which cost £45,000[WON]

— Barnston Lane School **Moreton** opened[WON]

— Open Golf Championship held at Royal Liverpool Golf Club Hoylake *(see opposite page)*[RLGC]

— Work commenced on the first section of the promenade extension from Marine Park **New Brighton** to Harrison Drive **Wallasey**[RPW]

— Carlton Players first performed in **Birkenhead**

Apr Work began on construction & widening of Leasowe Road – **Leasowe** to **Wallasey** Village

30 Sept **Wallasey** Golf Club Ladies pavilion opened. Cost £600[WGC]

30 Sept Death of FE Smith, Earl of **Birkenhead**, aged 59 - brilliant Statesman, Lawyer, Orator and Old Birkonian[OIH]

2 Oct Application granted for a golfing licence to the *Queens Picture House* Grange Road **West Kirby** *(see this page)*

1 Nov The first effort to raise funds to start the first training of Guide Dogs for the Blind in the UK was an Open Alsatian Dog Show at The Auditorium **Port Sunlight** *(see also Oct 1931)*

The Queens Picture House Grange Road **West Kirby** opened on 24 December 1921 in the building once the public hall. 0n 2 October 1930 an application was granted for a golfing licence at the cinema! The miniature golf course was built on the stage, partitioned off from the rest of the theatre but not interfering with the projection of films; it opened 24 November 1930. A round of the 18 holes cost 6d [2.5p] and took about half an hour – after a month the course record was 42. The bulk of the golf course was on the stage, the rest housed in the old green room and one of the numerous dressing rooms no longer used. The golfers could hear the films but the cinema goers could not hear the golfers! Some of the names given to the holes were Hilbre Caves; Dee Bridge; Halfway House & Beechers Brook

These tearooms were built in 1930 and called the 'Cottage Loaf' with the idea of supplying the public with homely comfort and old-fashioned baking and cooking in pleasant surroundings. The building itself is very picturesque and has a garden, with sunny lawns on which tea is served in the summer. All the bread, scones, and cakes served are made in our own kitchens and we make our own jam and lemon cheese. Eggs, milk and cream are supplied by local farms. Two minutes walk away is one of the beauty spots of the neighbourhood, Thurstaston Hill, from which some of the finest views in England may be seen. Thurstaston village itself is very beautiful and is well worth a visit.

This information was taken from a *Cottage Loaf* letter card when Mrs HF Simpson was the proprietor. The tearooms opened at **Thurstaston** on 21 December 1930. A 1933 advert states that dances were held every Tuesday & Friday throughout the Winter from 8pm to 12pm (evening dress desirable). On Dance nights the normal service was carried on in the Upstairs Tea Room

The spectators are watching the 1930 Open Championship at Royal Liverpool Golf Club in which Bobby Jones was the champion. The *Royal Hotel* in Stanley Road **Hoylake** is the large building in the background and was the original headquarters for the club until the present clubhouse was opened in 1895 [the hotel was demolished in 1958 and houses built on the site][RLGC]

Above: Parkgate Promenade taken before 1932 when Mostyn House School, the tall building on the right, incorporated its present black & white frontage. The *Union Hotel*, to the left of the man with a boater later became the *Ship Hotel* and Dee House on the extreme left was replaced with Nichols Famous Ice Cream Shop *and Post Office in 1935*[YW6]

Below: The *Ship Inn* 80 Market Street **Hoylake**, which was a public house owned by Birkenhead Brewery and dates back to at least 1820, is seen here *c.*1930 when the publican was John Richards. To the right of the main entrance is one of the Hoylake Fire Brigade's Fire Call alarms which was installed here and at the *Railway Inn* Meols in September 1912 where the glass could be broken in an emergency. The half-door entrance to the cellars is on the right[YW3]

— **Birkenhead** Junior School building, formerly Overdale, opened – presented to the school by Graham White MP *(see opposite)*[OIH]

— Mahler Memorial open-air annexe to Elleray Park School **New Brighton**

— Duke of Kent visited Cammell Laird shipyard **Birkenhead** and laid the keel of HMS Achilles[MOI]

— Municipal Self Service Laundry opened in Oakdale Road **Wallasey**[WON]

— **Hoylake** baths re-opened having been re-built *(see this page)*[YW3]

— **Thornton Hough** Women's Institute opened[YW8]

— One hundred houses on the Leasowe Road Estate **Moreton** completed. The prices for the three & four bedroom houses were £640 & £725 respectively

1 Jan   An offence for any person to drive a motor vehicle unless covered against third party risks

3 Mar   Bascule bridge opened between East & West Floats at Duke Street **Birkenhead**

14 April   Argyle Theatre **Birkenhead** became the first music hall to broadcast live on BBC Radio[RP]

17 April   **Bromborough** Dock opened - constructed by Lever Brothers

July   Birkenhead & District Co-op Society new dairy opened on Swan Hill, Woodchurch Road **Prenton**[BPH]

July   Widening & construction of Pasture Road **Moreton** to **Leasowe** including a new bridge over the railway costing £24,600[YW5]

26 Sept   Wirral Grammar School for Boys and Girls, **Bebington** both officially opened[YW8]

Oct   First four guide dogs for the blind in the UK return home from a makeshift training centre at **Wallasey** organised by Miss Muriel Crooke

12 Oct   Our Lady Star of the Sea opened in **Ellesmere Port**[DoS]

The *Argyle Theatre* Argyle Street **Birkenhead** became the first music hall to broadcast live on the radio direct from the theatre 14 April 1931 and later the first to be relayed to America. The single act of Leslie Strange was chosen for the first experimental broadcast and due to the tremendous fan mail that followed proving that the programme was a success, a series of relays from the *Argyle* was soon making the grade in the National and British Empire programmes

Above: Hoylake new baths re-built in 1931 and many English Championship races were held here in the 1930s. They were closed during the war and the ARP were stationed here[YW3]

Below: West Kirby Marine Lake is pictured in 1930. In February 1931 the local council borrowed £2,450 for construction of baths in West Kirby Lake and the bathing facilities improved. However a scheme to build a wall separating the baths from the lake was turned down in 1935 on grounds of cost *(see also 1935)*[YW3]

Below: There has been a windmill on **Bidston** Hill dating back to at least 1596. This was a wooden peg or post mill which was destroyed by fire in 1791. This present mill, which replaced the burnt one, operated until 1875 and was left to decay. However, it was restored in 1894 thanks to Robert Hudson, the soap manufacturer. Although its sails had to be replaced in 1927 and the 1970s, it still stands proud as a permanent landmark

This was a popular comic postcard theme using cats in a human situation. This one states "You 'AUTO' come here it's ripping! HOYLAKE

Above: *Overdale* which stands at the junction of Bidston Road & Beresford Road **Oxton** was presented to Birkenhead School by an old boy H Graham White MP. It was used then and is still used today to house Junior School[OIH]

Below: New Chester Road **Rock Ferry** with the policeman standing at the junction of Bedford Road. This was taken in February 1931 ten months before the tram service closed. The bus is a Leyland Titan DT1 No153 (Reg. No. BG201)[BB]

—	**Brimstage** Village Hall erected on the site of the Red Cat Inn[YW8]
—	New ss Royal Iris came into service at **Wallasey**
—	New Ferry baths opened
28 Feb	Queen's Picture House **West Kirby** burnt to the ground[YW3]
9 April	**Overchurch** Scout Hut opened (see below)
16 May	First Stableford Golf Competition held – at **Wallasey** Golf Club[YW5]
21 May	Foundation stone laid for the Harrison Memorial Hall **Wallasey Village**
21 May	The oil tanker *British Commander* collides into and destroys **Egremont** Ferry *(see next page)*[WON]
8 June	Derby Baths opened in Harrison Drive **Wallasey**. An open-air sea-water bath with accommodation for 1,000 bathers & 2,000 spectators[WON]
9 June	The new **Hoylake** lifeboat *Oldham* was christened by the ex-Mayer of Oldham Mrs Waterworth *(see this page)*[YW3]
30 July	Foundation stone laid for the R.C. Church of SS Peter & Paul **New Brighton**[DoS]
10 Aug	**Frankby** Hall Estate which comprised of 810 acres in Frankby, Greasby and Newton was up for auction. Frankby Hall *(see this page)* was withdrawn @ £5,000 but bought the following year for £12,500 by Wallasey Corporation for use as a cemetery

Overchurch Scout Hut opened 9 April 1932 at **Upton**. It was an anonomous gift for the Wallasey Boy Scouts as a camping ground

Wallasey Golf Club, which had been founded in 1891, is pictured here in 1932, the year in which the first Stableford Golf Competition ever held was at Wallasey Golf Club on 16 May. The founder of the Stableford system of scoring was Dr Frank Stableford, captain of Wallasey Golf Club in 1933

Frankby Hall which dates back to 1846/7 was home of the Royden family for generations. When the Frankby Hall Estate was up for auction 10 August 1932 the hall was withdrawn at £5,000 but an offer of £12,500 including 61 acres of land was later accepted from Wallasey Corporation. The corporation bought the estate for use as a cemetery as the Rake Lane Cemetery would have been full by 1953. The first internment here was 29 August 1940

The old and new transport systems of trams and buses are seen side by side at Woodside **Birkenhead** in 1932 with Woodside Station building in the background. The letter 'C' on the balcony rails of the No 23 tram was for the Circle route via Conway Street. The last tram ran 17 July 1937[TBW]

The first motor lifeboat at **Hoylake** the *Oldham* was named on 9 June 1932 by the ex-Mayer of Oldham Mrs Waterworth. She last saw service on 4 September 1951 and during her service had been launched 43 times and saved 20 lives

This picture postcard shows the damage caused to **Egremont** Ferry stage when a large oil tanker cut it in two. The message on the back of the card tells the story: *. . . remember this bridge in Egremont,. A ship ran through it a week or two ago and this is how it looks now . . . . people were on the stage waiting for the boat and had to be taken off in tugs.* On 21 May 1932 the oil tanker *British Commander* rammed Egremont Pier splitting it in two. The *Mammoth* floating crane lifted the 75ton bridge to West Float Dock in Birkenhead. It cost £7,340 to repair and the ferry was back in service by 1933 *(see also 1941)*

New Ferry baths were built on the Bebington Council's river frontage to the Mersey Bank Estate at a cost of £12,000 and opened in July 1932. During the first two months there were 80,000 visitors – bathers and non-bathers.

Described as one of the most up todate open-air swimming baths in the country, the dimensions of the rectangular bath were 330ft in length by 90ft wide with the depth varying from three to sixteen feet. The capacity of one million gallons was supplied with water drawn from the River Mersey by electric pump then forced up to filter beds of such a capacity that the water was thoroughly cleansed every 12 hours and after being chemically treated and aerated it was delivered to the shallow end. The baths were sold in the mid 1970s and a housing development now stands on the site

—   **Birkenhead** police took over the **Upton** District from Cheshire including Upton Police Station. Due to the increased area, police boxes were erected at Sparks Lane, Vyner Road and Overchurch Road. One was also placed in Pine Walks **Prenton**[MQP]

—   Hippodrome Cinema, Carnegie Street opened in **Ellesmere Port**[SSW2]

—   Grange Secondary school, Tollemache Road **Birkenhead** opened

27 Mar   Byrne Avenue Baths **Rock Ferry** opened

10 April   New terminus opened at **Seacombe** Ferry *(see opposite page)*[WON]

28 April   **Bidston** Dock opened

28 April   Borough of Birkenhead borders extended to include: **Arrowe, Upton, Woodchurch, Noctorum,** parts of **Bidston**[KD]

Aug   (Bank Holiday Monday) First Birkenhead & District Annual Sheep Dog Trials held in Rectory Fields **Woodchurch**

Sept   St Anselms College Manor Hill **Birkenhead** opened on the former site of Outwood *(see this page)*

Sept   *West Kirby Hotel* **West Kirby** changed its name to the *Hoylake Hotel*[YW3]

24 Sept   Christ the King R.C. Church opened in New Chester Road **Bromborough**[DOS]

3 Nov   Gaumont Cinema King Street **Wallasey** opened[SSW2]

30 Nov   Last **Wallasey** Corporation tram ran

1 Dec   **Wallasey** Tramways ended[TBW]

4 Dec   Tudor Cinema **West Kirby** opened *(see this page)*[SSW2]

The Tudor Cinema opened on the site of the Queens Picture House on the corner of Grange Road and Bridge Street **West Kirby** on 4 December 1933. The Queens had been destroyed by fire in 1932[SSW2]

St Anselms College, which is viewed from the main entrance in Manor Hill **Birkenhead** opened in September 1933. The house was formerly *Outwood*

Described on this postcard as "a small coaching cafe – all the food is home-made and very delicious" is the Devon Doorway. It was built in 1930 for a Devon lady Mrs Aldridge and situated at the junction of Barnston Road, Chester High Road and Telegraph Road **Heswall** which is why it was also an ideal site for the early RAC hut pictured on the left[YW6]

This postcard was produced to announce that the new entrance hall was officially opened at **Seacombe** Ferry 10 April 1933. The tram lines pictured here were still in use until Wallasey Corporation finally closed the tram system later that year on 30 November. Following this closure, the area in front of the terminus building was totally redesigned *(See 1934)*

This view of Derby Baths was taken in 1933 by Whitfield & Cannon of Wallasey the year after they were opened in Harrison Drive **Wallasey** on 8 June 1932 by Lord Derby. This open-air sea-water bath with accommodation for 1,000 bathers & 2,000 spectators was more popular with the locals than the New Brighton baths. This was a period of fashion change for men's swimwear – some are wearing the old-fashioned swim suits and some are bare chested[YW4]

— New road safety measures introduced including 'Belisha Beacons', traffic lights and the 30 mph speed limit

— New Dispensary erected in Mill Lane Hospital **Wallasey** equipped with modern X-Ray apparatus[MM]

— **Wallasey** Council opened Gorsedale Elementary School[WON]

— New ss *Royal Daffodil* comes into service at **Wallasey**[WCS]

— Large new Passenger Bridge installed at **New Brighton** Pier[RPW]

— **Landican** Cemetery opened in Arrowe Park Road

16 Mar   Submarine *Sealion* launched at Cammell Laird **Birkenhead**[MOI]

31 Mar   Good Friday. 66,500 walk through the new Mersey Tunnel between **Birkenhead** and Liverpool for charity prior to opening

12 May   Destroyer HMS *Fearless* launched at Cammell Laird **Birkenhead**[MOI]

30/31 May   Duke of York visited **Port Sunlight**[KD]

13 June   **New Brighton** Bathing Pool opened. Cost £95,000 - largest in the UK with accomodation for 2,000 bathers & 10,000 spectators. Almost one million paying customers visited the pool in the first four months[YW4]

13 June   Work started on the extension to **New Brighton** promenade

29 June   Destroyer HMS *Foresight* launched at Cammell Laird **Birkenhead**[MOI]

18 July   King George V and Queen Mary opened the Queensway Mersey Tunnel and the new library in Borough Road **Birkenhead** *(see this page)*[KD]

1 Aug   Rivacre open-air swimming pool opened at **Ellesmere Port**[EP]

22 Oct   Electricity Offices & Showrooms opened in Wallasey Road **Liscard**[WON]

24 Oct   Sacred Heart School **Moreton** opened – built at a cost of £10,000[DoS]

Rivacre Valley Swimming Pool between **Ellesmere Port** and **Little Sutton** opened 1 August 1934 within the Rivacre Valley's 45 acres of public open space. The diving pool area seen here was totally separate from the main swimming pool. Built at a cost of £12,000 it opened from May to September and was known as *the swimming pool in a garden*[YW9]

A booklet was produced to commemorate the Mersey Tunnel Ceremonial Inauguration by HRH Princess Mary Viscountess Lascelles 16 December 1925 in which appeared this artist's impression of a cross sectional view of the proposed tunnel. They visualised that the two outside lanes would be for horse-drawn transport and there would be people walking through the tunnel!

This aerial view of **Birkenhead** Docks and the River Mersey published in 1934, also shows **Seacombe** Ferry *(pictured below)* top left

This photograph was taken a year after the new entrance hall was officially opened at **Seacombe** Ferry 10 April 1933 and after the tram system closed on 30 November the same year. Following this closure, the area in front of the terminus building was totally redesigned (see 1933). The tram lines have been removed and the area where the taxis would await custom in the centre, facing the main entrance, has been landscaped[WB]

Left: This panaromic view was taken on the occasion of the opening of the Mersey Tunnel on 18 July 1934 at the **Birkenhead** entrance in King's Square. The crowds have gathered to watch King George V and Queen Mary perform the opening ceremony. Work had commenced both sides of the River Mersey on 16 December 1925, taking almost nine years to complete. Birkenhead Market is the long building on the left and the town hall clock stands to the right. The length of roadway of the main tunnel is 2.13 miles[BPH]

—	*Nelson Hotel* opened in Grove Road **Wallasey**
—	**Birkenhead** Co-op Society opened new premises in Grange Road on the site of the Hippodrome Theatre[YW7]
—	New houses on the Townfield Estate, Townfield Lane **Bebington** built by G Brereton offered for sale from £650 to £825[YW8]
—	Boulton's Sunshine Villas have eight developments on Wirral with houses from £550 to £975[YW8]
—	Nine hole municipal golf course opened at Brackenwood **Bebington**[YW8]
May	**Tranmere** Cross rediscovered being used as a sun dial having disappeared c.1862 *(see picture opposite)*[YW8]
6 May	King George V Silver Jubilee
June	**Birkenhead** Police had to deal with a disturbance between Dock Labourers and 'Blackshirts' (Fascists) in Park Street[MQP]
2 Aug	First Mass celebrated at SS Peter & Pauls RC Church **New Brighton** *(see picture opposite)*. The Church was built on the site of *Sandrock* which stood at the top of St Georges Mount[DoS]
Sept	The local council turned down a scheme to erect a wall between **West Kirby** swimming pool and Marine Lake due to the cost of £1,350[YW3]
25 Sept	**Birkenhead** Town Council rejected a proposal that a Corporation Bus service should operate through the Mersey Tunnel

BLACK HORSE HOTEL,
GRANGE HILL, WEST KIRBY.

THIS Hotel is situate on the Grange Hill, nestled under the gorse and heather in a most picturesque position. It commands extensive views of the greater portion of the Hundred of Wirral the Coast of North Wales, with the shores of Seaforth, Waterloo, Blundellsands, Formby, and the Bay of Liverpool, as well as distant views of the Hills of Lancashire.

It is only ten minutes' walk from the termini of the Wirral and Mersey and the L. & N. W. and G. W. Joint Railways.

Splendid Accommodation for Dinners and Pic-Nic Parties.

SANITATION PERFECT.

Special arrangements made for the enterment and comfort of Visitors.

Wines, Spirits and Cigars of the finest quality.

JOHN VAUGHAN,
Proprietor.

Above Right: An early advert for the *Black Horse Hotel* taken from an 1897 Hoylake & West Kirby Directory

Below: The *Black Horse Hotel*, is pictured in Black Horse Hill **West Kirby** January 1935. The original building built of stone is seen on the left with the new brick-built building to the right. The *Black Horse Inn* is mentioned in Philip Sulley's *The Hundred of Wirral* 1889 as the meeting place for the West Kirby Benevolent Society which was founded in 1828 and had 150 members. There was a *Chesnut Horse* public house listed at Grange in 1850 when Esther Ball was the victualler and by 1860 Wm Powell had taken over. This was possibly the original name for the *Black Horse*

Looking down Grange Road **Birkenhead** in 1935, Irwins Grocers shop is on the left next to FW Woolworths who later moved to new premises on the site of Grange Road Baptist Church on the corner of Catherine Street. The white building beyond is the Birkenhead Co-op Society's new premises opened in this year on the site of the Hippodrome Theatre[YW2]

Tranmere Cross which dates back to c.15th Century when it probably stood in Church Road Tranmere. It disappeared c.1862 and was re-discovered in May 1935 being used used as a sun dial in front of the main doorway to Tranmere New Hall. It was then presented by the last resident of Tranmere New Hall, Joseph Long, to the Parks Committee and was re-erected in Victoria Park Tranmere

REVO

England's Foremost Electric Cooker in your Home for **5/-** **per quarter.**

You cannot judge electric cooking without having first tried it. Once you have tried it you will never revert to old-fashioned methods. YOU CAN HIRE A REVO No. 2 ECONOMY COOKER for approximately 4½d. per week and operate it at a cost of 1d. per person per day!

See it on the stand of the

Birkenhead Corporation Electricity Dept.

REVO Electric Co., Ltd., Tipton

This advertisement was taken from a souvenir programme of the Birkenhead Municipal Exhibition held at the Drill Hall Grange Road West **Birkenhead** in 1935

Left: This is the Architect's drawing of St Peter & Paul RC Church **New Brighton** which was built on the site of *Sandrock* at the top of St Georges Mount and held its first Mass 2 August 1935[DoS]

—	**Heswall** Presbyterian Church of England, Telegraph Road purchased 1,140 sq yds of land - formerly part of Heswall Castle grounds[YW6]
—	St Philips Church opened at **Storeton**[YW8]
—	*Punch Bowl* public house Market Street **Hoylake** replaced with a new building and original one demolished *(see picture opposite)*[YW3]
—	**Upton** Library opened
—	First edition of ***Bebington*** News
20 Jan	King George V died
13 June	**Wallasey's** first Milk Bar opened at 132 Borough Road **Seacombe**
July	Dee Cottage at the junction of Dee Lane and Banks Road **West Kirby** was demolished followed by a road-widening scheme *(see this page)*[YW3]
17 Sept	**Irby** Methodist Church opened in Mill Hill Road. Prior to this the congregation used the 'Tin Chapel' opposite Irby Hill Farm and before 1881 the Primitive Methodists used the farmhouse

This photograph of Mill Hill Road **Irby** *c.*1936 shows the farmer taking his cows to be milked at a time when there were no pavements or road markings here and vehicular traffic was not a problem.

It was in this road that archaeologists found evidence of a working farm with crops and cattle dating from 200AD to 400AD including 13 buildings some of which were built on top of each other

Tor Right: The last area of sand at **Parkgate** is seen in the mid 1930s but it was not until after the Second World War that the sand finally disappeared under grass. The black & white timbered *Boathouse Cafe* in the background was built in 1926 on the site of the old coaching inn the *Pengwern Arms*, whose outbuildings can be seen on the left and were used as the headquarters for the local Boy Scouts until the building was demolished and the site developed as a car park

Centre Right: The *Horse & Jockey Inn* at Woodchurch is pictured in Upton Road **Woodchurch**. This Birkenhead Brewery pub being situated on a main road from Birkenhead to Upton, Greasby and beyond, was very popular with cyclists and also ramblers. It was at Arrowe Park opposite the inn that the International Scout Jamboree was held for two weeks in 1929 which must have brought an excellent business opportunity to the landlord Septimus Broster. He had been landlord since 1907 and died in this year 1936. It was in 1937 that the pub was replaced with the *Arrowe Park Hotel (see 1937)*[BPH]

Above: Dee Cottage is seen in Banks Road **West Kirby** at its junction with Dee Lane (off to the right) just before the building was demolished in July 1936 so that road widening improvements could be carried out. An old resident at this time remembered the tale of a lady who lived at Dee Cottage in the early 19th century a certain Nanny Houghton. She had two sons, one of whom married and left the district, the other was nicknamed 'daft Jack'. He murdered his mother and buried her in the garden and when enquiries were made, he admitted his guilt[YW3]

Right: The *Punch Bowl*, pictured to the left of the open car in Market Street, **Hoylake**, was the cause of a bottle neck for many years and was finally demolished in 1936 being replaced with the present building which was built behind the old pub

—	Eastway School opened at **Moreton**
—	**Tranmere** Cross re-erected in Victoria Park
—	**Irby** Village Hall erected at a cost of £1,600
—	Tutty's store in Oxton Road **Birkenhead** taken over by Rostances
—	*Swan Hotel* Holm Lane **Oxton** rebuilt c.1937
—	**Wallasey** Parish Church of St Marys Diamond Jubilee 1877–1937
—	*Central Hotel* Clifton Crescent **Birkenhead** opened; built by Lloyd & Cross
—	Arrowe Park Hotel **Woodchurch** replaced *Horse & Jockey Inn (see opposite)*
12 Feb	The 1,316 seater Regal Cinema opened (later Essoldo) in Bebington Road **Rock Ferry**
13 April	Aircraft carrier *Ark Royal* launched at Cammell Laird **Birkenhead**
10 May	King George V Memorial unveilled adjoining Central Library Borough Road **Birkenhead**
12 May	King George VI crowned
19 May	An RAF plane on a night flight from Sealand Nr Chester crash-landed into Marine Lake **West Kirby**. Although the aircraft turned 'turtle' with wheels uppermost, Pilot Officer Earle escaped unhurt
17 July	Last **Birkenhead** electric tram route closed
4 Oct	The new *Ritz Cinema* at the junction of Claughton Road and Oliver Street **Birkenhead** was opened by Gracie Fields as the "Showpiece of the North"
17 Oct	Bruce Ismay died
28 Sept	**Bebington** received its Royal Charter

Jean Black's Nestle Wave; Reynolds Surgical Trusses and Stroude's Drapers and Furnishers adverts were all taken from the Coronation Souvenir of Celebrations in **Wallasey** 1937

The *Arrowe Park Hotel* which replaced the *Horse & Jockey Inn (see1936)* and took its licence is seen at the junction of Upton Road and Church Lane **Woodchurch** – the AD 1937 date stone can be seen on the white gable ends[BPH]

Gayton Mill, in Telegraph Road **Gayton**, is seen in this pen & ink sketch of John Pride. The Miller's Cottage is to the left

Birkenhead Tramcar No 22 has been illuminated for this last sad day of the tram era which dated back to when Europe's first public tram system started in **Birkenhead** 1860. This illuminated tramcar had been used to celebrate the Coronation earlier in 1937 and had been retained for this its final role. Owen Murphy, the oldest driver who started with the horse-drawn tramcars of the Victorian era, was chosen for this final role. The sign on the side of the tram reads "Other Days – Other Ways"[BT]

The *Ark Royal* is pictured in January 1939 having been launched from Cammell Laird **Birkenhead** 13 April 1937. She was the first ship to be designed and built as an aircraft carrier, carrying 60 aircraft comprising Fairey Swordfish and Blackburn Skuas. She was involved in tracking down *Graff Spee* and also the Bismark. She was finally torpedoed and sank off Gibralt 14 November 1941[BPH]

— Overchurch Primary School Moreton Road **Upton** opened[YW5]

— **Birkenhead** Fire Station Whetstone Lane buildings extended to include married quarters[YW2]

4 Feb New YMCA building opened in Whetstone Lane **Birkenhead** built be Lloyd & Cross and opened by the Earl of Shrewsbury[SS]

Mar New Police Station building opened in Queens Road **Hoylake** replacing old one dating back to *c.1868 (see aerial view opposite)*[YW3]

30 May New *Gaumont Cinema* opened Park Road East **Birkenhead** showing I See Ice starring George Formby[GB]

24 July SS Mauretania launched at Cammell Laird **Birkenhead** (see below)[MOI]

This sketch of Village Road, **West Kirby** Village, by John Pride c.1938 shows the row of old cottages up from the Post Office. Instead of being demolished in the 1960/70s, they were sympathetically restored and add a charm to the area

This view of the Cunard ship SS *Mauretania* was taken in the River Mersey after her launch from Cammell Laird shipyard **Birkenhead** in July 1938. This 34,000 ton passenger liner was then the largest ship built in England, making her maiden voyage the following year *(see 1939)*[MOI]

This march-past took place in Hamilton Square **Birkenhead** 1938

Above: The *Grange Hotel* Hoylake Road **Moreton** at the junction of Acton Lane was granted planning permission March 1938 and was opened for Higson's Brewery May 1938. The advert for the opening described it as "The most beautiful hotel in the North of England"[YW5]

Right: The four men – one up a ladder and the other three on the roof are demolishing the original *Railway Inn* Birkenhead Road **Meols**. This was after the new one had been opened on 1 December 1938 behind the old site which now forms part of the car park. The first inhabitants of the new pub were a family of owls who gave the local residents a disturbed night[YW5]

Below: This aerial view of **Hoylake** was taken in 1938 when the Hoylake Police Station in Queens Road was being built. Other landmarks include: The Quadrant and *Stanley Hotel* in the foreground; Market Street as it heads off towards **Meols** in the distance; part of the railway line on the right and the swimming baths top left

—	Part of St Catherines Hospital in Church Road **Tranmere** became a military hospital
3 May	*Prince of Wales* launched at Cammell Laird **Birkenhead**[YW2]
1 June	Submarine *Thetis*, after leaving Cammell Laird shipyard **Birkenhead** for trials, sank off Anglesey. Of those on board, 99 died with only four survivers *(see opposite page)*[TAR]
17 June	SS *Mauretania* sailed on its maiden voyage to New York[MOI]
30 June	**Rock Ferry** ferry closed[WCS]
30 June	Lifeboat Station on **Hilbre Island** closed[YW3]
3 Sept	WAR DECLARED
	Birkenhead Police Force declared that following the outbreak of war and the introduction of the 'black–out', an increasing number of accidents were reported involving vehicles[MQP]
5 Nov	Our Lady and St John RC Church opened in Telegraph Road **Heswall**[DoS]
13 Nov	*Palace Cinema* New Chester Road **Rock Ferry** re-opened with the film *Stagecoach*[SSW1]
1Dec	**Birkenhead** General Hospital new Coronation Wing opened by Lord Leverhulme – built at a cost of £25,000[YW2]
15 Dec	Gift of an ambulance to the **Birkenhead** Red Cross Society in memory of Mr Robert Smith by his two sons

"Dainty Teas" were one Cafe Concord's specialities available at Banks Road **West Kirby** and they also catered for the Garden Pavilion Cafe in the gardens on West Kirby Promenade according to their advert in the Hoylake & West Kirby Official Guide of 1938/39

SS *Mauretania* is passing Fort Perch Rock **New Brighton** on her maiden voyage early summer 1939. This 34,000 passenger liner was used as a troop-carrier during the Second World War transporting over 350,000 troops and travelling over half a million miles[MOI]

Below: Rock Ferry ferry, pictured from the *Royal Rock Hotel*, closed 30 June 1939; Liverpool is seen across the River Mersey

The Birkenhead Philharmonic Society programme on 22 March 1939 contained the following two advertisements:
Above: The *Royal Rock Hotel* **Rock Ferry** and
Left: The Birkenhead Automobile Company of Woodchurch Road and Briardale Road **Birkenhead**

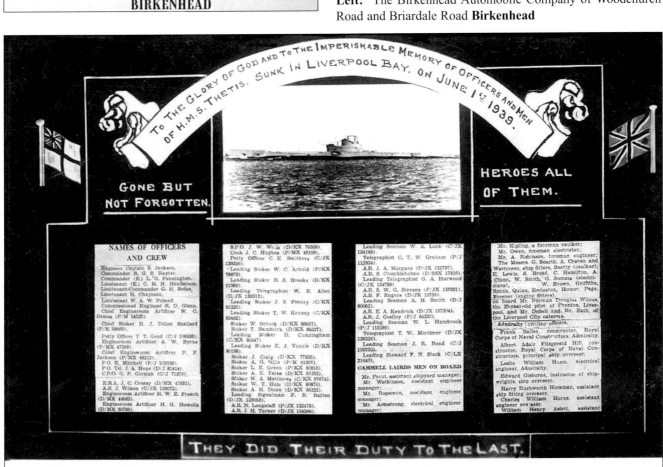

This postcard was issued in memory of the 99 men that died on the Cammell Laird built submarine HMS *Thetis* during sea trials off Anglesey [for more information see *Thetis - The Admiralty Regrets* and *HMS Thetis - Secrets & Scandal* – Avid Publications]

—	**Wallasey** Golf Club links requisitioned for war purposes[WAW]
—	**Wallasey** Corporation. opened new cemetry at **Frankby**
—	Railings around **Birkenhead** Park salvaged for war effort
4 May	New Fire Station opened Telegraph Road **Heswall** – total cost £13,000 – £14,000
10 May	EVACUATION of DUNKIRK commenced
14 May	National Local Defence Volunteers formed[CHG]
23 May	First parade of **West Kirby** & **Hoylake** Area LDV held at Caldy GGS[TRA]
June	Evacuees from Guernsey arrive at **Irby** *(see opposite page)*
23 July	LDV became known as Home Guard[CHG]
9 Aug	First bombs dropped locally – on **Prenton**
10 Aug	First air raid on **Wallasey**[WAW]
29 Aug	King George & Queen Elizabeth visit Cammell Laird **Birkenhead**
21 Sept	Argyle Theatre **Birkenhead** suffered a direct hit during bombing raid and was destroyed[WTB]
29 Sept	Slatey Road Police station **Birkenhead** suffered bomb damage and was later demolished[WTB]
29 Sept	Allansons' store Grange Road **Birkenhead** damaged by incendiary bomb
8 Oct	German Junkers bomber plane shot down near **Bromborough** Dock
5/6Nov	King George & Queen Elizabeth visit bombed areas in Wallasey and **Birkenhead**[WAW]

The new fire headquarters in telegraph Road **Heswall** opened on 4 May 1940. Built on the site of two houses at a cost between £13,000 & £14,000 (including the land). Prior to this station opening they had to rely on **Birkenhead** Fire Brigade turning out but due to war conditions they could not receive any guarantee of help

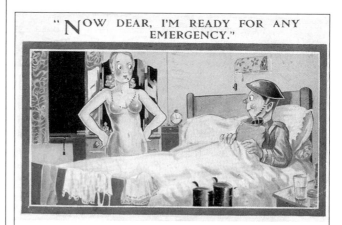

A comic war-time postcard published by "Humoresque"

Following an attack 26/27 September 1940 on the LMS/GWR marshalling yard in **Birkenhead** a burning ammunition train was saved from blowing up by the brave efforts of George Tunna who was subsequently awarded the George Cross[CHG]

A group of firemen from the NFS standing in front of their fire engine at **Ellesmere Port**

THE HOME GUARD

Following a broadcast for volunteers on 14th May 1940, by the then secretary of State for War, the Right Honourable Anthony Eden, the Local Defence Volunteer movement was formed. On 23rd July 1940 the LDV became the Home Guard and by early summer of 1943 nationwide there were 1,100 battalions with 43,000 officers and over two million men.

The 4th Cheshire (Birkenhead) Battalion Home Guard was formed at the Plaza Cinema **Birkenhead** on 28 May 1940 when over 1,000 men enrolled. This is a group from the **Bidston** Home Guard which was No 6 Company (of six) of the Battalion initially under the command of H Russell Edwards. In July 1940 Bidston became No. 2 Company (of five) with L Wynne Evans as their commander. This picture shows the cross-section of ages; from the young on the front row, with the Brigade's dog, to the older ones at the back, who probably fought in the First World War[CHG]

GUERNSEY EVACUEES

Following the fall of Paris on 12 June 1940 and the imminent fall of the rest of France, the German occupation of the Channel Islands became inevitable. There was voluntary evacuation to Britain of the civilians where 34,500 residents of a population of 100,000 left before the surrender on 1 July 1940. This included many children who were kept together in their school groups with St Andrew's School Guernsey with their teachers, Lester Robilliard, Peter Cherry, Winifred Woodgate and Mabel Le Pelley being evacuated to Irby via Manchester. One of the children was Marion Enevoldsen (see picture right) who lined up with the others in Irby Parish Hall waiting to find out who would be their hosts – as it turned out for the next five years. Muriel and Eric Boumphrey [the author's parents] already had an 18 month boy and wanted a younger girl rather than a teenager and so they were Marion's guardians for the next five years. The children stayed together as a group with their school lessons being held in the Methodist Church Hall in Mill Lane. As well as the good times there were painful moments; not knowing for 18 months what had become of her parents back on the island due to no letters being allowed either to or from the island. Then Marion was permitted to send a letter limited to 25 words.

After the Germans surrendered the Channel Islands in May 1945, the evacuees returned home later that year

*Marion Enevoldsen, an evacuee from Guernsey, is pictured in her 'guardians'' garden in Glenwood Drive **Irby** June 1945 with their son Brian [the author's brother]*
(see this page)

12 Mar	288 were killed in **Birkenhead** on night of 12/13 March[BCSB]
12 Mar	The *Caernarvon Castle* Bidston Road **Oxton** was destroyed due to a land mine falling behind the pub[WTB]
12 Mar	Start of a three day bombing campaign over Merseyside - over 10,000 homeless in **Wallasey**[WAW]
14 Mar	Colliseum Cinema **Wallasey Village** received a direct hit from a German bomb[WAW]
Mar	During March 186 people were killed in **Wallasey**[WAW]
25 Apr	Winston Churchill paid suprise visit to **Birkenhead** and **Wallasey**[WAW]
21 May	The training ship *HMS Conway* which was moored in the Mersey off **Rock Ferry** left her moorings and sailed to the safer waters of the the Menai Straits *(see page opposite & also 1953)*[TC]
21 July	**Birkenhead** luggage ferry service discontinued
18 Aug	All fire Brigades nationalised[FPH]
13 Nov	Built by **Birkenhead** shipbuilder Cammell Laird, the aircraft carrier *Ark Royal* was torpedoed off Gibraltar *(see opposite)*
10 Dec	Cammell Laird built Battleship *Prince of Wales* torpedoed and sunk off Malaya

Damage incurred to Brattan Road **Birkenhead** following an air raid on the night of the 12/13 March 1941. This was the night that a mine dropped behind the Caernarvon Castle in Bidston Road **Oxton** which demolished the pub and caused severe damage to the roof of St Saviour's Church nearby. Over 270 groups of incendiary bombs, 300 high explosive bombs and 60 parachute mines exploded in the Birkenhead and Wallasey areas. On this and the following night a total of 631 people were killed and a similar number injured in Merseyside[WTB]

A member of the **Wallasey** National Fire Service, Harold Jones, is seen standing in one of their fire-fighting vehicles on his Wedding Day 21 August 1941. His bride, Lorna Smart is climbing the ladder. The NFS was a voluntary service; Harold was a ship broker by day and fire fighter by night

Above: Two Anderson Shelters belonging to 6 & 8 Lynwood Avenue **Wallasey** are pictured following an air raid on 10 August 1940. The official report describes them as 'unmasked' shelters pierced by shrapnel *(see details of Anderson Shelters below)*

Above: Training Ship HMS *Conway* moored in the Menai Straits off the shore base of *Plas Newydd* (acquired in 1949) with their rugby pitch in the foreground[TC]

Left: The bowler-hatted gentleman is standing amidst rubble following an air raid attack on **Wallasey** and in front of an Anderson Shelter which has survived the attack. Anderson Shelters were named after Sir John Anderson, Cabinet Minister in charge of ARP, and became a familiar sight in gardens throughout the area. They were cheap to produce, made from six corrugated steel sheets bolted together at the top with steel plates either end and measuring 6ft 6in x 4ft 6in. The shelter was then 'planted' three feet into the ground and covered with at least 18 inches of earth.   Up to six people could be protected from almost anything but a direct hit. Over two million were distributed free of charge before October 1939 but then anyone earning over £5 a week had to buy their own at prices ranging from £6.14s to £10.18s. Production ceased in March 1940 due partly to a steel shortage but also by then the use of communal shelters was officially encouraged[SAW]

The training ship HMS *Conway* was based in the River Mersey off **Rock Ferry** at the outbreak of war in 1939. During an air raid on 12 November 1940 a 13,000 ton whale-factory ship, SS Hektoria, with a full cargo on board, dragged her anchors and collided with the *Conway*. The training ship spent the next four months in Vittoria Dock **Birkenhead** being repaired then returned to her moorings. During a night raid in March 1941, two parachute mines were dropped near *Conway* and the SS *Tacoma City* anchored nearby. The cadets were evacuated to accommodation in Rock Ferry save for the boat crew and some staff who remained on board. The following day one of the mines sank *Tacoma City* her crew being rescued by *Conway's* boat. The other mine was subsequently exploded by a mine sweeper. The cadets were then moved to Mostyn House School at **Parkgate** pending finding a safer mooring. A berth was found off Bangor in the Menai Straits, North Wales. At 3pm on 21 May 1941 she prepared to leave the Mersey in tow of the *Langworth and Dongarth*. The journey to her new berth took nine hours *(see also 1953)*[TC]

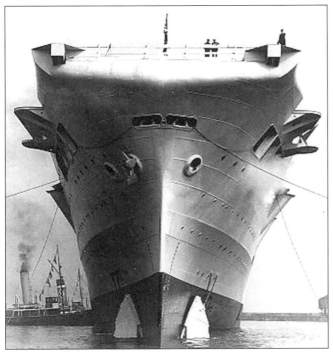

Left: The order for the new *Ark Royal* was placed with Cammell Laird **Birkenhead** and work on the £2,330,000 contract started in 1935. She took two years to build and was launched 13 April 1937. This ship of 22,000 tons was the first purpose built aircraft carrier with a flight deck of 800 feet in length and 94 feet beam. She carried a compliment of 1,575 officers and men, 60 aircraft and had a speed of 30.75 knots. She was fitted out just in time to join hostilities when war broke out in september 1939. One of her first duties was to take part in the destruction of the French Fleet at Oran. Her supreme achievement was the attack on the *Bismark* when her aircraft slowed down this German Battleship and enabled the British battleships to get in range and sink her with their heavy guns. The *Ark Royal* was herself torpedoed 13 November 1941and sank off Gibralta.
Queen Elizabeth launched the new *Ark Royal* at Cammell Laird **Birkenhead** on 3 May 1950.

Jan	**Birkenhead** was the top area nationwide for collecting waste paper
Jan	Mr George Arnold Cherry was appointed as **Birkenhead** Transport Manager
10 Jan	Last bomb fell on MerseysideWAW
Mar	Caves under **New Brighton** Promenade converted into munition factory *(see this page)*
Mar	National Warship Week. Towns in Wirral to sponsor warships:– **Birkenhead** raised over £1,500,000 for HMS *Charybdis*; **Bebington** raised £236,000 for MHS *Sabre*; **Hoylake** raised £428,208 for HMS *Verdun*; **Ellesmere Port** raised £173,000 for HMS *Espiegle*, Wirral (**Heswall** & District) raised £150,346 for HMS *Ophelia* and **Neston** raised £99,000 for HMS Motor Torpedo Boat 87
16 Apr	George Cross awarded to Malta
3 May	Death of Mr AK Bulley founder of **Ness** Gardens
23 Oct to 3 Nov	Battle of El Alamein

Below: Workmen sinking a stanchion for a new roundabout on **New Brighton** Promenade uncovered caves which gave Mr W Wilkie amusement director of the Palace Amusements the idea of starting a munitions factory there. Following development to provide blast-proof rooms, production commenced in March 1942. Unknown to millions of holiday-makers, beneath the promenade the weekly output of this small factory was up to 250,000 machine-gun bullets, 25,000 shells and 1,400 press-button switches for aircraft radios

A. R. P.
All - Right - Presently

DOWN THE 'OLE!
OUR 'OLE'S A NICE 'OLE
SNUG AND TIGHT –
COME DOWN IN OUR 'OLE
AND YOU'LL BE ALRIGHT.

THE 'OLE

Above: This postcard of the West Kirby Tennis Tournament was posted in 1942. Pictured in the Upper Park **West Kirby**, St Bridgets Church can be seen in the centre horizon

Left: A war-time comic postcard encouraging people to use air raid shelters. Initially many would not use them even in high risk areas such as **Birkenhead** or **Wallasey**. However, after a few nights of bombing many more reluctantly made use of them

Below: One of the most demanding and dangerous jobs during the war was that of the Bomb Disposal Team. This group of them is pictured with a bomb in **Wallasey** and shows how, once the detonator has been removed, the bomb can be hoisted clear of obstructions with the help of a rig

— The railings from Puddydale School **Heswall** were removed for salvage[SOP]

31 Jan Remnants of the 6th German Army surrender at Stalingrad

6 Feb Bronze medals awarded to two **Hoylake** lifeboatmen – Herbert Jones and Ben Armitage and a Coastguard Officer– WJ Widdup who used a rowing boat to rescue two occupants of a dinghy[HLA]

3 Sept Allies invade Italy

Nov Due to lack of war-time labour several boys from Puddydale School **Heswall** were excused school in order to pick potatoes[SOP]

I'll be back again after the war, meanwhile –

Use my STORK COOKERY SERVICE
MORE QUICK-TO-MAKE PUDDINGS

DON'T skip the sweet course, as some people do these days; families badly need the extra energy and nourishment provided by a pudding; besides, sweets supply most of the meal's variety nowadays. The new Stork Leaflet No. 62 gives some excellent recipes for new puddings—some light, some substantial, all easy to make. So send the coupon for your free copy now. All recipes approved by Ministry of Food.

STORK MARGARINE COOKERY SERVICE

Top: War-time advertisement for Stork Margerine

Above: The "B" Company of the 17th Cheshire (Heswall) Battalion Home Guard are pictured in the playground of the Puddydale School in Dale Avenue **Heswall**. As early as September 1939, there were six air raid shelters dug into the ground on the Puddydale for the use of the children[SOP]

Left: This Salvage Week display was in Irwins' [later to become Tesco] shop window Pensby Road **Heswall**. It was to encourage public awareness of the need to save waste paper and other salvage to help fund the war effort

20 May	Start of Wirral UDC 'Salute the Soldier Week' 20 to 27 May. The district's target was £150,000 which would cover the cost of equipping and clothing three Parachute Battalions. Centres were at **Heswall, Barnston, Irby & Pensby**
6 June	D Day Allied landing in Normandy
Aug	Puddydale School **Heswall** took 38 evacuees from London & Southern Counties[SOP]
8 Sept	First V2 Rocket–bomb fell in England

Above: Members of the **Hoylake** UDC, with the leader Mr SV Tomkinson on the left, are seen standing in Market Street **Hoylake** by a poster which is behind the wall of the *Stanley Hotel*. The caricature of 'Monty' and the map of Normandy dates this poster, requesting magazines for the soldiers at the front, at 1944

Right: This war-time comic postcard depicting a scantilly-clad girl wearing a Warden's helmet was to encourage the population to keep calm in troubled times!

Below: The No. 2 Platoon "A" Company 17th Battalion Cheshire Regiment Home Guard are posing at the rear of the Royal Liverpool Golf Club in Meols Drive **Hoylake**. This was their parade ground and Headquarters. They were also known as the "Green Lodge Crowd" as this is where they held their first meetings and probably had the occasional drink there as well[RAA]

—	St Anslem's College, Manor Hill **Birkenhead** became a Direct Grant Grammar School[DOS]		floodlighting of public buildings, bonfires, Parades *(see picture opposite)* and Mersey River Cruises on illuminated ferryboat[WVC]
—	Mount Estate **Bebington** started built by Lloyd & Cross	4 Sept	Victory dances at **New Brighton** Tower Ballroom for six nights[WVC]
8 May	VE (Victory in Europe) – Day Celebrations. The town halls of **Birkenhead, Wallasey, Neston** and **Hoylake** were decorated with flags and bunting *(see below)*[WVC]	14/21 Sept	Victory Dances at three halls in **Moreton**[WVC]
15/17 May	Victory Dances at **New Brighton** Tower Ballroom[WVC]	23 Sept	Orchestral Concert at Moreton Picture House, Pasture Road **Moreton** as part of the Victory Celebrations[WVC]
16 May	Victory Dances at three halls in **Moreton**[WVC]	11 Oct	Final Victory dance at **New Brighton** Tower Ballroom[WVC]
6 Aug	First Atom Bomb dropped on Hiroshima in Japan	29 Nov	Isle of Man steamer *King Orry* launched at Cammell Laird **Birkenhead** [WCS]
9 Aug	Atom Bomb dropped on Nagasaki		
14 Aug	Japan surrenders to the Allies	Dec	School children at Puddydale School **Heswall** were given an extra two days holiday at Christmas as part of victory celebrations[SOTP]
15 Aug	VJ (Victory in Japan) Day. End of war celebrations across Wirral – Music by bands,		

Above: The Royal Observer Corps men who were stationed at the Upper Lighthouse in **Hoylake** are seen passing in front of Hoylake Town Hall in Market Street. Norman Ellison, the well known local broadcaster & writer, is the left of the two men leading the parade (he was deputy-head Observer), which was to celebrate VE Day 8 May 1945. A group of local dignitaries are taking the march past from a raised platform in front of the Town Hall entrance

Right: The band is leading the procession along the same route as pictured above in **Hoylake**. This time the celebration is the final end of the war following the surrender of Japan to the Allies on 14 August 1945

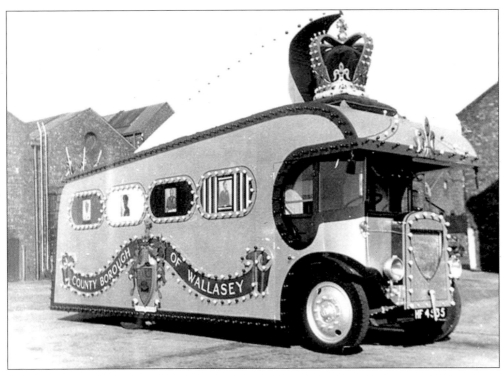

This Leyland Lion PLSC1 Reg No HF4535 (fleet No 8) started with the **Wallasey** bus fleet in 1927 and was withdrawn in 1941. In 1945 it was converted into an illuminated bus and is seen here commemorating the end of the war. It was also used for other events including the Festival of Britain in 1951 and the Coronation of 1953. It was sold to Morris and Pulford in 1954 and used as a contractors site office. Parts of it were used in the restoration of a similar vehicle by Ribble Motor Services[TWB]

—	Vernon's Industries erected purpose built industrial units in Valley Road **Birkenhead**
8 June	All children receive a certificate from King George VI *(see below)*
9 Aug	The 1946 Wirral District Dance Band Championship held at Tower Ballroom **New Brighton** *(see this page)*

TOWER BALLROOM
New Brighton

LEWIS BUCKLEY presents
under the auspices of the "MELODY MAKER"

The 1946 WIRRAL DISTRICT
DANCE BAND
CHAMPIONSHIP

FRIDAY, AUGUST 9th

DANCING 7 p.m. to 11-45 p.m.

LATE FERRY TO SEACOMBE AND LIVERPOOL. 12 P.M

House Band
Bert Yates and His Tower Rhythmics

TICKETS 3/-: FORCES 2/-

SOUVENIR PROGRAMME

8th June, 1946

To-day, as we celebrate victory, I send this personal message to you and all other boys and girls at school. For you have shared in the hardships and dangers of a total war and you have shared no less in the triumph of the Allied Nations.

I know you will always feel proud to belong to a country which was capable of such supreme effort; proud, too, of parents and elder brothers and sisters who by their courage, endurance and enterprise brought victory. May these qualities be yours as you grow up and join in the common effort to establish among the nations of the world unity and peace.

George R.I.

This certificate was issued to all children on 8 June 1946 with a personal message from King George VI thanking them for sharing in the hardships and dangers of war

Top Left: This view of the Tower Grounds show that **New Brighton** is returning to its pre-war popularity

Above: This is the cover of the programme for the 1946 Wirral District Dance Band championship held at the Tower Ballroom **New Brighton** under the auspices of the *Melody Maker*. The winner having the chance to compete in the area final and the winners of each area final to compete in the national final. The bands competing were: Tommy Crompton and His Band from Eastham, Bobby Nick's Swingtette from Liverpool, George Cobb and his Swingtette from Runcorn, Art Dickens and his Band from Northwich, The Deva Quintette from Chester, Ron Hall and his Band from Wigan, Fred Higham and his Band from Warrington and The Aldo-Hawkins Septette from Widnes

Above: This photograph of the Promenade at **Parkgate** was taken just post-war. By the corner of the building on the right is a black and white post which would warn drivers or riders of the building, which could not be seen in the black-out during the war. The pavement and kerb stones on the left are painted white for the same reason. The River Dee is just starting to silt up and it was beyond the Boathouse Cafe, centre background, that the last sand was seen at Parkgate about this time

Below: The Wall of death at **New Brighton** dates back to 1930. Jack Roche, who rode the Wall of Death as 'Jack Campbell' at New Brighton Tower Grounds from 1947 to 1951, is standing by his Indian Scout motorbike. Using a microphone he is advertising the attraction, with Maureen Swift riding her bike on rollers to give the spectators a sense of excitement from the noise of the bike together with the smell of the fumes. The public would then pay their entrance fee, climb the steps and look down from the top circle onto the Wall of Death. After the show it was customary to ask the audience to throw money into the centre as a tip to allow for the fact that Wall of Death riders could not get any insurance cover. This show was operated by Bill Miller at New Brighton until 1959 when it moved to Southend-on-Sea and then to Kenya. Following a serious accident in 1953, Jack never rode the wall again

— Williams & Williams Ltd of Chester opened a factory in the former buildings of the Royal Ordnance Factory in **Hooton**, calling it 'Roften'. They produced kitchen and bath units for Government owned 'pre–fab' bungalows. These were built to overcome the housing shortage – some of these estates were built locally on spare land including at Wolverham and Stud Farm *(see also 1949 for pre–fabs)*[EP]

— **Arrowe** Park Golf Course used in the qualifying rounds of the British Open Championship[BCSB]

— Both companies of Odex Ltd & Racasan Ltd came from Liverpool and set up business in **Ellesmere Port** on land formerly owned by Wolverhampton Corrugated Iron Company[EP]

Aug　British Open Championship held at Royal Liverpool Golf Club **Hoylake**. Won by Irishman Fred Daly[RLGC2]

Oct　Building commenced on the **Woodchurch** Estate

20 Nov　Royal Wedding of Princess Elizabeth to Prince Philip

Below: Holiday makers and day trippers are seen enjoying themselves on the beach in post-war **New Brighton**. The pier in the background was just one of many attractions to delight the public. Others included the New Brighton Tower and grounds with many amusements and rides, the boating lake, the many theatres and cinemas and not forgetting the largest outdoor baths in Europe

Bottom: Looking across to Liverpool from **New Brighton** beach shows one of the ferry boats which transported thousands of day trippers across the Mersey. The vehicle on the right was an amphibious vehicle known as a 'DUKW' – a remnant of the war left behind by the Americans – and used here to give rides along the beach

- Tommy Mann's Enterprises Miniature Railway opened on **New Brighton** Promenade (see this page)[UTKR]
- Railway system nationalised under British Rail
- Jackson Earle's first "Melody Inn Revue" at the Floral Pavilion **New Brighton** which was to run for a record breaking 25 years
- Mackie & Gladstone wine & spirit merchants of **Birkenhead** taken over by Birkenhead Brewery

2 Feb   Foundation stone laid for new Electricity Power Station at **Bromborough**

1 April   Denationalisation of the Fire Service. Re-established under Local Authority control[FPH]

5 July   Fire Service & Ambulance Service combine in **Birkenhead**. Fire Brigade personel increased to 122. Firemen now employed on 60 hour week[FPH]

21 Aug   **Wallasey** Civic Week held from 21st to 28th

15 Oct   New **Irby** Village Hall opened

Left: In post-war **New Brighton** the proprietors of the New Brighton Tower launched the "Tower's Special Effort" to bring the Nazi atrocities in the Belsen and Buchenwald concentration camps to the public attention by exposing their horrors. A poster tells us that all proceeds from this exhibition were for local charities.

Below: Tommy Mann's Enterprises Miniature Railway, also known as the Fairy Glen Miniature Railway, opened on **New Brighton** Promenade in 1948. The line was installed by Tommy Mann who also ran the Marine Lake on the Promenade at New Brighton. He bought equipment from the former 18 inch gauge Jaywick Railway, near Clacton on Sea, Essex which had closed down after war broke out in 1939. In 1950 another locomotive was purchased and in 1952 a new canopied station was built. The railway ran at New Brighton until the end of the 1965 season.

—	Raby House Girls Boarding School opened at **Willaston**
—	Rationing ended
6 May	First council house on **Woodchurch** Estate formally opened
29 Sept	Building work commenced on the **Birkenhead** technical College in Borough Road **Birkenhead**
21 Nov	Royal Film Performance at Ritz Theatre **Birkenhead** showing *The Forsyte Saga*. The Band & Trumpeters of the 22nd Cheshire Regiment provided the live music

Bromborough Cross has been retained although the centre of the village has kept up with modern demands by building new shops for an increasing population. The base and steps of the cross probably date back to late *c*.13 with a new shaft and canopied head being added in 1874. Labourers could be hired out from here and the village market would be held within sight of the cross. The *Royal Oak* public house, which can be seen to the right of the cross, is said to date back to the time of Charles I. Due to increased demand the pub became too small so a new, much larger one was built to the left of the shops and the licence transfered, opening in 1958[YW9]

Towards the end of the war it was anticipated that there would be a national shortage of housing, particularly in areas like Merseyside which had suffered from enemy bombing during the war and it could not be solved entirely by normal building methods. The term 'prefab' was first used in 1944 when Lord Portal, Minister of Works in the National Government, conceived a scheme for one storey prefabricated steel houses which could also use female labour. However, as the price of steel rose the alternative material utilised was aluminium with a weather-proofing finish. This scheme, which produced nationally owned housing at a reasonable rent, was only intended as a temporary measure with the buildings having an estimated maximum life of ten years. These prefabs pictured were in Molyneux Road on the **Upton/Greasby** border sited between Greasby Road and Arrowe Park Road. The single storey buildings survived much longer than the maximum ten years envisaged, with many people not wanting to leave what had been for some of them their home for upwards of thirty years. Frankby Grove and Molyneux Close occupy this area today[STS]

—	**Birkenhead** Brewery acquired the business of Moorhouse Bros Ltd; one of Merseyside's leading mineral water manufacturers
3 May	Queen Elizabeth launched the aircraft carrier *Ark Royal* at Cammell Laird **Birkenhead** and laid the Foundation Stone for **Birkenhead** Technical College in Borough Road
7 Aug	The Annual **Heswall** Horse & Horticultural Show held on the Glegg Estate land at Gayton *(see opposite page)*
Dec	The first time **Birkenhead's** senior Police Officers have their photograph taken as a group and appears in a local newspaper *(see below)*

Below:-

Birkenhead's Police Officers photographed December 1950 with the Chief Constable are:–

Seated left to right: Inspector Harold Marchant, Chief Inspector Kenneth Maxwell, Chief Inspector Edward M Morris, Superintendent William K Ellis, the Deputy Chief Constable Superintendent Walter R Jones, Chief Constable Henry J Vann, Superintendent Robert Tankard, Chief Inspector Benjamin Williams, Detective Chief Inspector Louis J Caldwell (head of the CID), Inspector Tom I Griffiths.

Standing left to right: Inspectors Stanley Blundell, Thomas R Appleton, TE Lloyd Roberts, John Gallagher, William A Williamson, William GL Johnston, Andrew M McIntosh, Laurence R Allsop, Fred Berry and Henry E Thomas. One officer, Chief Inspector Thomas J Oliver, was away serving with the Control Commission in Germany.

Work on the building of Birkenhead Technical College Borough Road **Birkenhead** started 29 September 1949 and the foundation stone laid by Queen Elizabeth on 3 May 1950. Design was by Willink and Dod and the building was estimated to be completed in three years at a cost of £653,000. The top photograph shows the shell with the completed college shown below (which opened in 1955). The Queen launched the new aircraft carrier *Ark Royal* at **Birkenhead** shipyard of Cammell Laird on the same day

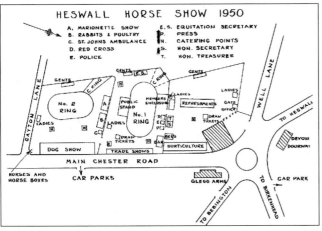

The annual **Heswall** & District Horse & Agricultural Show was held on land at **Gayton** belonging to the Glegg Estate on 7 August 1950. The location was in the field opposite the *Glegg Arms* and is shown on the map above taken from the programme. Also in the programme was an advertisement for the Glegg Estate Development Co Ltd *(see this page)* which stated that the show was held on part of their 140 acre estate and was all prime building land. They were offering their services to anyone wanting to develop on this site.

The entertainments on the day included Horse & Gymkhana events; an Horticultural Show with 116 classes, a Dog Show, Rabbit Show, Marionette Show, Honey Show, display by the British Alsation Training Club, music and entertainment by the Pipers & Dancers of the Liverpool Scottish (TA) and Trade Shows. Unfortunately the Poultry Show had to be cancelled due to an outbreak of Fowl Pest in the area.

—	Guiness Clock sited on **New Brighton** Promenade to celebrate the Festival of Britain *(see this page)*
—	**Wallasey** Corporation Diesel-electric ferry boat *Royal Iris* entered service
—	**Birkenhead** Co-operative Society celebrated their centenary
Mar	**Birkenhead** Amateur Operatic Society celebrated its Silver Jubilee with a performance of *Showboat*
Apr	Carlton Players of **Birkenhead** celebrated their 21st Birthday
22 May	First big post-war Gang Show performed for two nights at the Tower Ballroom **New Brighton**
25 Aug	The Festival of Britain Birkenhead Horse Show and Gymkhana was the first of 20 to be held annually at the Old Birkonian Rugby Club ground at **Noctorum**[FOBB]
1 Sept	Official opening of Old Parkonian's Ground Holm Lane **Oxton** – HA Fry's Lancashire XV v LB (Losh) Smith's Cheshire XV[FOBB]
4 Sept	Festival of Britain ship Campania arrived at Bidston Dock **Birkenhead** where she was open to public viewing from 5th until 14th September *(see opposite)*[FOBB]
8/9 Sept	Scout Jamborette at **Arrowe Park**[FOBB]
3 Dec	Storeton Station on the Bidston to Wrexham railway line closed to passengers[PWR]

Above: The Guinness Festival Clock, which was created for the Festival of Britain Pleasure Gardens in Battersea Park, London, was said to be 25 feet high. Seven of them were produced and sited in other parts of the country including one pictured here in the Tower Grounds facing the Promenade at **New Brighton**. Every fifteen minutes the clock would burst into life: the sun spun round, the keeper rose from under an umbrella, the ostrich emerged from a chimney, marionettes revolved around a whirlygig, the Mad Hatter came out of his house, and, finally, two toucans came out to peck at a Guinness Time Tree. All this took about five minutes so the clock was in action every ten minutes and drew large crowds. This one at New Brighton operated until at least 1960[BGA]

In 1947 the Government decided that the centenary of the Great Exhibition of 1851 should be marked by national displays. These would demonstrate to the world the British advances in science, technology, industrial design, as well as the arts and architecture. Battersea Park in London was chosen as the centrepiece for the Festival with displays in other cities around the United Kingdom. The former ferry carrier HMS Campania was chosen as a floating exhibition that would visit ten ports around the country from May to October 1951. She was converted into a miniature version of the South Bank Exhibition at Cammell Laird shipyard Birkenhead. Local people could visit the ship when she visited Bidston Dock **Birkenhead** from 4 to 14 September 1951[FSC]

—	New RC Church 'Our Lady of Pity' opened in Mill Lane **Greasby**[SDYB]	—	Birkenhead School's 'McAllester Memorial Ground' Bidston Road **Oxton** officially opened donated by GL in memory of his brother [LCOIH]
—	Wallasey ferry boat Egremont built for either ferrying up to 1,472 passengers on the **Seacombe** to Liverpool route or carrying 700 on river cruise[WCS]	7 Feb	King George VI dies
		8 Dec	First Japanese ship to enter the Mersey since the war

Above: Hoylake Baths, which can be seen in the foreground of this aerial view of **Hoylake** promenade, were originally opened in June 1913 and rebuilt in 1931. Many English Championships were held here in the 1930s. With the outbreak of war the baths were closed and the ARP stationed here. Taken over in 1976 by the Hoylake Pool & Community Trust it was demolished in 1984 [YW3]

Below: Birkenhead Town Hall can be seen in the background and the market to the left of this photograph taken from the main Birkenhead entrance to the Mersey Tunnel. The tunnel charges then were very complex especially for private cars which were charged according to horse-power and the number and ages of passengers. A car under 8 HP was 1/- (one shilling) [5p], 8 to 12 HP was 1/6 [7.5p], over12 hp was 2/- [10p]. However, charges were also made for passengers at 2d [1p] each or children under 14 at 1d. Therefore a car exceeding 12 HP with four passengers aged over 14 would pay 2/8d [13.5p] which would be more than the charge for a lorry exceeding 4 tons @ 2/6 [12.5p]! A steam propelled goods vehicle was 2/6d and a steam roller would be 5/- [25p]. An ambulance was charged at 2/- and a bicycle was 3d [1p] or bicycle and side-car 6d [2.5p]. Even circuses were not left out – a "showman's special vehicle" was charged at 2/6d *(taken from 'Mersey Tunnel Schedule of Tolls for Motor Vehicles etc 1951/52')*

14 Apr	Training ship HMS Conway on her way from Anglesey to be overhauled and refitted in dry-dock at **Birkenhead** slipped her moorings and became beached on the Caernarvon side of the Menai Straits close to the Suspension Bridge *(see this page, also 1941)*[TC]
22 May	Coronation cup & saucer distributed to schools in **Ellesmere Port**[EPCS]
30 May	HM Submarines *Artful* and *Seneschal* open to the public in **Birkenhead** Docks[BCSB]
30 May	Illuminations switched on in Hamilton Square **Birkenhead** prior to the Coronation celebrations[BCSB]
2 June	Queen Elizabeth II Coronation[BCSB]
4 June	Rivacre Pool **Ellesmere Port** Coronation Gala[EPCS]
31 Aug	Opening of English Martyrs Church **Wallasey**
3 Sept	Centenary Anniversary of the first **Birkenhead** *Advertiser (see this page)*
30 Oct	New **Birkenhead** Police Headquarters opened

Left: This stone statue stood in Manor Road **Upton** for many years which mysteriously disappeared

Below: This unusual view of **Birkenhead** was taken from above the main entrance looking towards Market Place South. Following heavy congestion, especially in the morning, a new approaches scheme was approved in 1966

A picture of Queen Elizabeth is seen on the wall of the Charles Thompson Mission in Hemingford Street **Birkenhead**. Watched by an audience of parents and friends, the children are enacting out the crowning of the "Mission Queen" as part of their celebrations for the Coronation which took place on 2 June 1953. This was a momentous year for the Mission as Annie Thompson, who was the superintendent, was awarded the MBE for her services to the poor children of Birkenhead. It was her father who had established the Mission in Hemingford Street back in 1892. When he died in 1903, Annie took over the running of the Mission until her death in 1956. In 1968 the Mission was incorporated into the Liverpool City Mission and although conditions have changed for the better, there is still a need for this important charity which still carries on their good work today[YW7]

The training ship HMS *Conway* is seen beached on the Caernarvon side of the Menai Straits near the Suspension Bridge. The ship was originally moored in the River Mersey off **Rock Ferry** but due to the air raids over Merseyside was moved to the Menai Straits in May 1942. It was decided that she needed an overhaul and refit so she was being towed to Bangor on 14 April 1953 for the first part of her journey by the tugs *Dongarth* and *Minegarth* when she was checked by the turn of a violent tide and a fairly fresh northerly wind. Under the strain, one of the towing lines parted and the ship gently took the ground – as seen in the photograph. The following day it was agreed that she could not be saved and was declared a total loss[TC]

INDEX

Please Note: Index references are to last two digits in year date – not page numbers ie. 52 = 1952 or 96 = 1896

Please Note: Index references are to last two digits in year date – not page numbers ie. 52 = 1952 or 96 = 1896

Please Note: Index references are to last two digits in year date – not page numbers ie. 52 = 1952 or 96 = 1896